This book is NOT a safe space

The unintended harm of political correctness

Corinna Fales

ISBN: 978-1-6847-1640-1 (sc)
ISBN: 978-1-6847-1639-5 (e)

Cover design by Carolyn Letvin, Letvin Design
Cover illustration by Laura Marshall, LauraMarshall.com
Interior drawing by Corinna Fales

Lulu Publishing Services rev. date: 01/21/2020

It is essential to have safe spaces, but it is not good for every space to be safe. Home should be safe. A therapist's office should be safe. But life is not safe. A continually safe space, in the wrong place, is very dangerous: It will stop you from growing and becoming.

For Joy & Bob;
for kids in the projects;
for everyone who has been living their life too small because of fear;
and for us all

CONTENTS

INTRODUCTION

This may initially appear to be an autobiography, but that is not my purpose in sharing parts of my life with you. My purpose is to demonstrate how and why I developed my unexpected understanding that political correctness (PC) creates unintended harm—a point of view that evolved from doing some deep and disagreeable work on myself. During that work, I unearthed in myself the presence of a mindset that had been vastly destructive to me and that, as I see it, underlies PC.

PC is a loaded, heavy, heated topic. The only way I know how to stimulate open, new dialogue about it is to address it in a heartfelt, personal way, with candor, humor, and forthrightness—not with some harangue or abstract theory. Besides, this is how I have had to go about it because it's just who I am.

I hope there is enough funniness here to keep you laughing. I want to shed new light on PC, not contribute to a fight.

1
WHO AM I TO TALK?

Someone screamed—a raw, raging cry.

"Fifty years! Isn't it enough!?"

It seemed far away, yet oddly nearby.

I was bewildered.

Then I realized it was me. And I knew exactly what I was screaming about.

That's how my therapeutic work with Joy began. Years of psychoanalysis had not even come close to touching that place in my soul, which unexpectedly detonated while I lay on a mat on the floor, breathing deeply to access whatever needed to emerge.

Without forethought, intention, or even awareness that I was thinking about it, I suddenly heard myself screaming about the fifty years I had spent trying to pay for my existence. So many people on both sides of my family had been murdered. Yet *I* was alive, *and* I was only a girl. How could I ever make up for my presence on Earth? I could exist, but I wasn't supposed to be happy. I was supposed to suffer, and I couldn't be successful. I wasn't supposed to have anything too good, do anything too cool. I apologized, for everything and nothing, all the time. I felt that I was living, as a character in the film *Dangerous Beauty* called it, "a life of perpetual inconsequence." I had not been slaughtered, but I had to become a victim, too. That's how I paid for being alive.

My role was to be the sacrificial lamb on the altar that my parents created as homage to the families they lost to the Nazis. I learned—very

1

well and very early—to sacrifice myself before anyone else could. At least I tried to, though it was mostly an unconscious, knee-jerk reaction. I was not aware of it as the guiding principle of my life till I screamed that day on a mat in Boston.

That was over twenty years ago, and through the years of therapeutic work that followed with Joy and her son Bob (each gifted in their own way and both very private people, so I will not identify them), I came to understand that my family's history, and their response to it, was a big chunk of the reason that I identified as a victim. I wasn't even aware that I felt like a victim because that would have been shameful: I was raised with Black folks (my friends prefer "Black"), who endure clear and terrible abuses every day. Their evident circumstances were (and are) so much harder than mine. The source of *my* suffering was veiled, subtle, unknown; and my parents did not talk about their past.

My mother's entire immediate family—mother, father, sister, and brother-in-law—were killed in a concentration camp. She was the sole survivor, and she transmitted her guilt about that (and her overwhelming anxiety) to me. I was supposed to carry it for her, or at least help her carry it; and I did so, as children do out of love and fear of abandonment.

My brother, being a boy, was the golden child. I think (and he may think differently) that he was largely exempt from the burden of guilt for our mother's survival—and, for that matter, our father's survival, because most of my father's family had been murdered, too. My brother was the family hope. He was supposed to carry on the family name and follow in our father's academic footsteps, which he did, and admirably. I don't know if he felt his role in the family to be a burden (or even a role), but I've never had that sense from him. At least it was an honor, and he was considered super smart and was expected to do well.

When my brother was nine and I was eight, our father died. That left our mother with two young children in a country she had escaped to with virtually nothing but her husband, eighteen years her senior and her former teacher, whom she virtually worshipped. Moreover, our father had been able to provide for us by working as a professor at Lincoln University, the first historically Black college/university in the country, while her German teaching credentials were not honored in the U.S.

A month after our father's death from cancer, we had to move out of faculty housing on Lincoln's campus and lost our home and our beloved community. After a long year of homelessness (during which another family thankfully took us in), my mother finally found a ramshackle old house she could afford to rent in the adjoining poor community known as the Village, and we moved to the "wrong" side of the tracks, where she fought with the landlord to get us an indoor bathroom.

It would have been much easier for my mother if I had died instead of my father.

But I didn't.

So then there was that, too.

From nine to thirteen, I slowly learned to navigate my radically different world with the help of a wonderful neighbor and friend. At thirteen, when I was in the tenth grade, my mother sent me away to boarding school. She had sent my brother a year earlier. Both of us got scholarships to good Quaker schools, which my mother said would help with future college acceptance. That was true. But I lost my home—again—and was thrown into a totally alien environment with a lot of rich and sophisticated White kids (and some less rich and less sophisticated ones, virtually all of whom were, however, White).

I was just a country girl, and I was used to being around Black people. I felt like a fish out of water.

In high school, you want to fit in. So I was excited when I went into town one Saturday and saw a tiny little dog—a Chihuahua. I had read about them and seen photos, and they seemed very fancy and were always with fancy people. I was so excited to have a perfect opportunity to show off how sophisticated I really was! When I got back to my dorm hall, I proudly announced that I had seen a CHEE **WHO**-a **WHO**-a in town. The girls looked at each other, puzzled. After what seemed like forever, one dryly said, "Ohhhh, a Chi-**WA**-wa." How do you make lemonade out of *that*? I crack up whenever I think of it.

When I graduated from high school at sixteen, my mother sent me to live in Germany for a year.

Please don't ask me why.

It broke me.

I became seriously suicidal, gained fifty pounds, bathed twice in ten months and washed my hair once, and developed polyps on my vocal chords from dealing with the crazy family I was living with and from trying to get my mother to hear that I needed to come home. But she made it quite clear that I could not come home before I was due to. When I was seventeen and still in Germany, I wrote a bitter poem that began, "To hear the cry locked deep in solitary throat cords..." and drew this internal self-portrait.

Three months after I got back to the U.S., I was set to begin college, which I had desperately clung to as the one thing that might somehow be meaningful and make life bearable again. I especially looked forward to having a roommate because I was so lonely and still suicidal that I was afraid I might start screaming and not stop. Then I received a letter from the school that I had been assigned a single room, and when I told my mother that I wanted to request a roommate (the school required her permission), she said I could not go to college unless I stayed in the single room. If I had some problem with being alone, she sternly said, I was to deal with it by being alone.

My first night in the dorm, it took everything in me to keep from dragging my mattress into the hall to sleep. I couldn't bear to be shut in that room by myself, and I only managed to keep from screaming because I knew that someone would haul me away. It was torture, and the nights that followed were no better. I drew lots of very dark pictures of people and wrote tormented poems.

And slowly grew furious.

Throughout college and after, I had the worst arguments with my mother that I have ever seen a mother and daughter have. But I channeled some of my rage—and simply who I am as a person—into work for the growing civil-rights movement (which led me to quit college after my sophomore year). Freedom rides and sit-ins, going to jail with like-minded friends—those made sense to me and slowly began to restore meaning to my life. I developed hope and purpose; I gradually re-developed passion.

In my early twenties, I described myself as a person who was encased in thick layers of bandages. I knew that I was not presenting my real self to the world. But I really didn't know who I was. I wasn't available to anyone, including myself. I simply couldn't afford it. I had made myself so small and created such a deep (*but unapparent*) disconnect from others, that I no longer knew who I was or what I was capable of. I always had the sense that I was someone else, really, but I mostly rolled along on automatic pilot as the miniaturized version of myself that I had come to know as me. The person underneath all those layers was in many ways a mystery—and apologized a thousand times a day, everywhere she went.

It might sound like I was false or fake. But I was never intentionally false or fake. I had just played myself so small that I no longer knew who I was. And if it seemed that someone else might "see" me—an exposure I could not afford—I fled (as happened when my T'ai Chi teacher told me that I responded more intuitively to another person's energy than anyone he had met, and I abruptly quit T'ai Chi). I wanted to be recognized but feared the consequences. And had no idea that my life was based on survivor guilt—until the day I screamed in Boston.

It's painful, embarrassing, and scary to write this. I put it off till I had written almost everything else for this book and couldn't even remember why I had ever thought I needed to say anything about myself, let alone what that was. I couldn't remember why I had ever felt like a victim. And I am still struggling with what is OK to tell and what is not: it is not my intention to hurt anyone, so I am giving you only a taste of what I went through. But my understanding of political correctness (PC) as victim-based and as having devastating consequences for people flows directly from what I have learned in my own life. This is personal—*it has always been personal*—I was just more resistant to it than I expected to be.

And I only now realized that I couldn't write about myself before because I had forgotten about self-love (which also means that I had forsaken my love for everyone else who considers themselves a victim). I had been feeling only shame about my victim identification and didn't want to divulge anything about myself. But loving myself through something I dislike in myself—understanding and appreciating the reason for its presence in me and how it has served me—is essential, and it's the only way I have ever been able to let go of it and change. That's part of what I've learned from my work with Joy and Bob, and it has enabled me to get to where I am today.

Feeling like a victim comes from pain. There is no joy in it. I am (emphatically) **not** denying or minimizing the atrocities that have always been part of the human landscape and are integral to our time on Earth and an ongoing part of our history. To the contrary. People have been subjugated, enslaved, raped, marginalized, degraded, oppressed, discriminated against, violated, murdered, humiliated, and annihilated. There are many, many reasons for people to feel like victims. I am not blaming them or you or myself for doing so. It is only *because* of our reality that victim is even a word or an issue.

My point is that it isn't good for us to identify as a victim. It is *never* good for us. All the people I know who have managed to overcome dreadful circumstances have in common that they did not identify as a victim, despite those circumstances. We must learn to acknowledge the reality of people's pain without giving them a victim identity.

"What?!" you say. "How are they *not* victims?"

Stay tuned.

For now, I want to say that designating individuals and groups as victims is at the heart of PC and is what makes PC inherently limiting, false, and unloving. That's what I have come to understand—through my personal life as a victim and my political life as an advocate for subjugated people—and that's what this book is about.

So here I am, after a lifelong and ongoing struggle to value and become my self, and to let go of my victim identity. If I can use what I have learned to help others, the misery I caused myself and the misery I didn't will have meaning.

And that's a lotta lemonade.

2
MEAT ME IN NEWARK

In 1968, I was thrown into Cook County Jail.

To get there—and believe me, there was a "there" there—I followed a road that began early in 1965, when I moved into one of the poor Black neighborhoods in Newark, N.J., to work as a community organizer. Please bear with me for a minute while I tell you how that road took me from Newark to Cook County Jail in Chicago. I will need to begin with an essay, "Jack's Meat Market" (copied below), which I wrote years later when I was living in Harlem and reflecting on my Newark experiences. Even before "Jack's," though, the years I spent working on my first book *(Different: Our Universal Longing for Community, 2016)* had begun to change my thinking about PC. The Black and White people I interviewed—who grew up in the same community I did and range from a prominent civil rights leader to the son of the county boss, who was widely reputed to be a member of the KKK—were honest and forthright and open in a way that was so different from PC, and such a gift! Then, writing "Jack's Meat Market" added to my growing frustration with PC.

JACK'S MEAT MARKET

Three of us White girls warily eyed the butcher. We had gone to Englewood, an affluent community in New Jersey, to find cheap sources of good meat for hundreds of Black women in nearby Newark. And we had reason to believe that he would only talk straight to other Whites about the sides of beef he had advertised.

"How does the quality of your meat compare to a supermarket's?" I asked. "That depends entirely on where you shop," he replied. "In Englewood or other suburbs, you're likely to get prime or choice. But in a Newark supermarket, you'll get only commercial grade—if that."

I had lived in Black communities most of my life and knew firsthand how bad the meat was in Newark. But I was still stunned when the butcher said that meat was intentionally segregated before it even left the warehouse.

I told some well-meaning White friends what he said, and they invariably replied that the meat was divided because low-income Blacks could not afford the better grades. What they did not and could not know, because they had not lived it, was that the abominable green meat in Newark's supermarkets was more expensive than the good, fresh meat in Englewood. So they must also have thought that the meat problem could not be fixed until the poverty problem was. But industry can be regulated, and regulations can be enforced.

We girls left Newark that day looking for meat because the community organization we worked with had shut down Jack's Meat Market, the only store where mothers on welfare could get credit, and hundreds of families were left without a way to feed their children.

Jack had an "arrangement" with caseworkers at the local welfare board. When women applied for assistance, the caseworkers told them to go to Jack's because he would extend them credit until they received their first check. And when Christmas rolled around, Jack gave the caseworkers some very nice gifts.

By the time their first check arrived, the women were already a month in arrears to Jack. And he used cereal as filler in his chopped meat, tipped the scales with his hands, didn't mark the prices on his goods, and had the highest prices in town.

The Black men who worked for him spilled these beans to us, though they feared for their jobs. We sent "spies," who confirmed their allegations—then organized a picket line and were joined by hundreds of welfare recipients.

No one crossed that line, and Jack abruptly folded. The men who worked for him lost their jobs but were proud, and the women needed a way to feed their children till their next check came.

We mobilized suburban friends, got donations of food, and tried to create a cooperative food chain that would offer mothers better value and savings going forward. As part of that effort, three of us White girls drove to Englewood and heard what the butcher had to say.

And now, whenever I hear the customary line about the cycle of poverty being caused by the poor, I think about Jack and those caseworkers. And I think about all the things we think we know, though we haven't lived them.

I also think about the number branded into Jack's forearm, which he got in a concentration camp. Since I am the daughter of Jews who barely survived the Nazis, I think about the fact that I did not hesitate to shut Jack down.

It was incomprehensible to me that someone who had suffered from prejudice would treat other people so cruelly. But I guess that Jack considered Black folks on welfare sub-human, like the Nazis had considered him. He just picked on people who are among the pariahs of our society and kicked his pain and pariah status down the social ladder.

That was in 1966, the year before Newark blew up. Several years later, I slumbered for a few decades while I lived a mostly White life in a mostly White community, and imperceptibly became one of the White people who only know what we are supposed to know and think what we are supposed to think.

Now I live in Harlem. People have lost the hope for change they had in the '60s. Gentrification is destroying their communities. And 103 teenagers who lived across the street from me in public housing were arrested last summer for alleged gang activity.

That raid woke me up, and I began working with kids in public housing to tell their stories. They live with constant danger and have learned to hide their tenderness, their hurt. They stay cool and hard, barely there, thin as ghosts. They know we don't believe in them and that they don't matter.

They are the pariahs now, those bad kids in the projects.
I have fallen in love with them.

***

Working with those kids got me to thinking about PC, and what we have and haven't changed. The projects have "gotten a bad name," so I was told to call them "housing developments."

Really?!

That makes them a better place to live, shows respect and sensitivity?

I think it's a straight-up PC-type of insult in the guise of caring—a denial of the reality of projects, which are warehouses for Black and Brown (and some White) people who aren't expected to go anywhere or become anything worthwhile.

Projects are the direct result of governmental policies at federal, state, and local levels that intentionally segregated housing and legally enforced its segregation (see *The Color of Law*, Richard Rothstein; W.W. Norton 2017). The kids in the projects across the street from me lost the programs and activities they had in the '60s and '70s, and spent years without basic services and programs, let alone lead abatement (as finally became public knowledge). However, the City spends *many* thousands of dollars on programs and policies on transgender issues. I am not knocking transgender folks—I am simply pointing out what every student of policy knows: our values determine the allocation of our resources. And no value is placed on those "bad kids" in the projects.

I have been a lifelong advocate for inclusion. As a friend's favorite t-shirt reads: "God loves everyone. No exceptions."

That needs to include the kids in the projects. Not just PC crushes.

***

In 1968, I had to leave Newark because the Black Power movement was in full swing and because people were in a rage from their treatment by Whites and the National Guard during the 1967 uprising, which took the lives of 26 people and injured hundreds more. Little kids who didn't know me furtively threw pebbles at me.

I didn't want to leave, but it was necessary and right. It was the time of Black Power.

I drove to California with friends—then back to Chicago to join a big demonstration against the Vietnam War at the Democratic National Convention.

And that's when I landed in Cook County Jail.

3
COOK COUNTY JAIL

As unsafe spaces go, Cook County Jail is the least safe space I have ever inhabited. It was more terrifying than going into East Berlin alone at sixteen, when the Berlin Wall was still up and not a soul in the world would know what had become of me if I disappeared. Far more terrifying than brain surgery, when I was cut from one ear to the other; or sleeping in the bathtub of my Newark apartment during the 1967 uprising to avoid getting hit by the National Guard's bullets whizzing around; or the time a White truck driver tried to run us over during a Freedom Ride on Route 40 in Maryland.

For fear, Cook County easily takes the cake.

By 1968, I had been arrested three times for civil-rights sit-ins and protests. I was proud of them and had never been scared. But Cook County scared the crap out of me. And I was only there because I sacrificed myself, not because I believed in what I did that put me there.

I have been trying to show you why feeling like a victim is not good for us. However, if you are determined to feel like one, here's a tip: self-sacrifice is a surefire and efficient way to do that. (You can even try this at home. People do it all the time.)

Cook County was my last arrest and the only one I am not proud of. Threatened with beatings, rape, and a sentence of twenty-five years, I had only put myself in harm's way to impress a man—a man I had worked with in Newark—and then doubled-down on that for a friend who might well not have done the same for me. I will never know.

When you lose your integrity and sacrifice yourself for something you don't believe in and are not proud of, you'd better learn something from it, and you'd better be prepared for the consequences because it is totally different from taking a risk for something you know is right.

Here's how I landed in Cook County—embarrassing to tell and much harder to have lived. I tried not to include it, but it kept knocking loudly on my brain to let it into this book, so I finally figured it belonged here for some reason unknown to me, and as I wrote it, I understood.

Most of the time in Chicago, I was at the headquarters of the anti-war demonstration, working on logistics. But after the police teargassed demonstrators in the streets, the guy I mentioned asked a few of us women (all women, of course) if we would be willing "to bring the teargas inside" the hotels where the convention delegates were housed and the meetings were held. He said women could more easily get past security.

I volunteered because he was a big cheese to us, and I wanted him to think I was cool. Besides, I didn't want to be the one woman in that tiny, select group who refused. But I thought it was a silly, stupid, meaningless thing to do. It was not like me at all—not my style of protest—and it made me very uncomfortable.

It also turned out to be a helluva way to get my mug shot in the *Chicago Tribune* (August 31, 1968).

Three of us went to a club in the Palmer House in Chicago with vials of butyric acid in our purses (butyric acid smells like vomit), and one spilled it onto the carpet beneath the table where we sat.

A couple of large men immediately popped up out of nowhere and took her away. But they completely disregarded the other two of us (they must not have realized that we were together).

We split up and went separate ways.

I could have gotten away if I had just left—but no—I sat down in the lobby of the hotel, trying to decide what to do about my vial of butyric acid and my friend who had gotten caught. I felt guilty that I was free (and so, perhaps, did the other woman who got away, because we both ended up getting caught).

And then, just as I made a half-hearted, undecided move to leave,

I spied a Newark judge in whose court I had appeared for one of my arrests; apparently, he was a convention delegate from New Jersey. I was enraged that he should represent *anyone,* and spun around, went back toward the Palmer House, and ducked into the women's room, where I emptied my butyric acid in a large planter—as if that were an act of real retribution for the judge's wrongs, and as if he used the ladies' room! Ridiculous, but I felt I couldn't leave without emptying my vial.

Then I went back to see what had happened to my friend, found the room where they were holding her, and peered inside. Yep, I stood there peering, like an idiot. And, of course, that's when I got arrested.

They separated us for questioning. The D.A. threatened to beat me with rubber hoses (because they don't leave marks, he said), he gleefully told me what the female inmates would do to us, and he read off the list of felony charges he intended to press that would get us twenty-five to life.

I was stone-faced. I hated him too much to show fear or say a word. *You can do anything you want to me*, I thought, *I will not crack.*

They threw us in the jail.

I had always been able to talk to anyone because I am genuinely interested in people, I don't judge them, and I don't think I'm better than anyone else. I had nothing against these inmates (all of whom, as I recall, were Black and overtly lesbian). I wasn't scared. They were not alien to me.

Only they were.

They were huge, they were cold, they were predators, and they were tough as hell—by far the roughest women I have ever met. They lived in a completely open cellblock with no walls. *Everything* they did was visible, all day and all night, 24/7.

If you had any humanity when you got to Cook County, that place would have stripped you of it, just to survive.

I tried talking to one woman who was having her hair done by another inmate. She just shot back that they were going to get me after lockdown that night. So, nope, I did not have a conversation with her, or with any of the other inmates.

Fear does not describe what I felt.

And there was nothing I could do to defend myself. The guards heard everything that was going on and laughed.

Then, suddenly, twenty minutes before lockdown for the night, we were told that some Chicago liberals had bailed the three of us out. I have never been so grateful, before or since. It still runs my blood cold to think what a night in that place would have cost me.

We were charged as unindicted co-conspirators of the "Chicago Seven." And when we had to appear in court, the guy who had put us up to all this—indicted as one of the "Chicago Seven"—laughed at my obvious terror at facing the judge. I thought that authorities could do anything to me. That mother-f had not grown up in my family or had his family murdered by an authoritarian regime.

Cook County was a terrifying lesson about myself and about friends. I will not sacrifice myself again for any, so-called, of those. Or anyone.

I once asked Bob why lessons have to be so hard.

He said, "So they stick."

Cook County stuck.

4
STUPID IS AS STUPID DOES

When I got out of Cook County, it suddenly dawned on me that I hadn't given a lick of thought to the next step of my life. Having to leave Newark was so painful for me that I hadn't focused on the future.

I suddenly had nowhere to go.

So, when a group of protestors asked if I wanted a ride to New York, I simply said OK and got in the car. That's how I got to where I spent the next fifty years in a place I never belonged.

I landed on the Lower East Side of Manhattan—at that time, a funky, poor, druggy community, now gentrifying—and soon thereafter met Buz, who later became my husband. After some months, Buz and I began living together in the sixth-floor rear apartment of a tenement.

As I told you in "Jack's," I learned a lot of things in Newark that White folks aren't supposed to know. My White relatives wouldn't even drive anywhere near the neighborhood where I lived, but I walked home by myself late at night and thought nothing of it. I had no fear (or good sense, my Black friends say). I was loved and protected and felt honored to be able to live there—those years were some of the most joyous and fulfilling of my life (which is intended in no way to diminish the dreadfulness of what people there went through).

I deeply loved most of the people I got to know in Newark—many of whom have since died, some of whom I am still in touch with. They ranged from those who would be considered "good," like hardworking families, to those who would be considered "bad," like mothers on welfare who had children by several men.

Ongoing brutality was visited on many of them by everyone from the welfare board to the police (who, for example, chained one sixteen-year-old friend to a radiator and beat her; we could hear it through the walls of our office, which was next to the precinct). What I witnessed in Newark was so horrendous that I came to believe that White people only accused Black folks of criminal behavior because they were racist. I believed that *any* Black person accused of *any* crime by *any* White person was innocent. I'm not referring to our historic and heinous unequal application of the law—which is a whole other topic—just to the idea that any White person *truthfully* accused *any* Black person of a crime.

I had my own PC world before PC. I thought it was based on fact.

Now, there's a famous line in the movie *Forrest Gump*: "Stupid is as stupid does." In this case, that would be me. When we ignore our gut because we are afraid of being racist or some other form of not-PC, we can be very stupid. (We can also be very stupid when we are trying to be PC and mean well, but don't understand that our words or actions are racist.)

One summer afternoon, Buz and I came home to our unlocked building, and two Black guys followed us into the hallway. As we picked up our mail, they loud-talked each other about buzzing their friend upstairs and whether he would be at home, etc.—in other words, they practically shouted that they were going to mug us. But we paid them no mind, partly because we were focused on our own conversation and partly because I knew that Black people didn't commit crimes. (Not against *me*, at any rate. Oh, the conceit.)

Anyway, after we got our mail, Buz and I sauntered up the stairs, chatting, blah blah blah, and the guys ran past us and waited on the landing above. When we got there, they jumped us. One put a knife to Buz's neck—the other threatened me with brass knuckles. I wasn't scared, and I wasn't about to give them my little bit of money. I don't know what Buz told the guy with the knife, but I told Mr. Brass Knuckles that I didn't have any money.

They told us to take them to our apartment, apparently to get what money they thought we kept there. Five flights up, we finally walked into our rear-facing apartment, and the guy with the knife went over to our windows and cut the ties on the curtains.

They closed with a soft, creepy swish. My heart sank.

I thought, *it's curtains for us.*

And it was my fault for refusing to give up my money. I knew that the guy who had a knife on Buz (let's call him Jimmy) was very dangerous, while the guy who was on me (let's call him Roy) still had some heart.

So I knew I had to talk fast to make some personal connection with Roy because Jimmy had taken Buz into the bedroom, and I had no idea what was happening. But I knew enough to be concerned for his life.

I told Roy that he shouldn't be robbing people like me—I only made $28 a week—he should rob my fancy boss on Madison Avenue. He said he would be happy to do that if I would help him. I said a bunch of other things that I don't remember, and then I asked him what his friend was going to do to Buz. He said he didn't know and asked me if I needed Buz.

Needed Buz? *Oh, hell no!* I thought.

I was a badass and a feminist. I didn't *need anybody*!

I dodged the question—said maybe I loved Buz.

Roy looked annoyed and impatient and started lecturing me: *Why was I shacking up with my boyfriend if I loved and needed him? When you love and need somebody, you should get married!* He kept asking me what the hell I was thinking by not getting married.

He gave me a freaking morals lecture!

Oh yes he did.

We all have our principles.

Then Jimmy came back with Buz and some rope and told Buz and me to sit on the couch. He and Roy tied up our feet. By then, I'd had the sense to fork over my little money, and I told them to leave me enough for "carfare" (as we used to call money for the subway) so I could get to work on Monday. They did. I also said that the ropes on my feet were too tight. They loosened them. Plus, Roy told me to remember what he said about getting married. Then they said they would kill us if we called the cops or anyone else—and left.

I breathed.

According to my friend Carol (a White friend I worked with in Newark), I told her that I just thought of Jesse M. while we were being mugged. Jesse was a fun guy we knew in Newark who claimed to be a bank robber (I never believed him), and Carol said I told her that I just talked to Roy as if he were Jesse. I don't remember, but it makes sense.

A Black friend of mine roared when I told her this story and said that I had changed Roy's life forever. He certainly changed mine.

That day, I learned to pay attention to my gut and trust my instincts. And a month or so later, I out-ran a pack of four guys up the six flights of stairs to my apartment, *wearing clogs.* Oh yes I did. I had paid attention on the street and knew they were going to come after me, so I got a running head start through the open front door and up the stairs. By the time I got to my apartment, panting wildly, they were right behind me. I frantically banged on the door, screaming *let me in!* A drowsy male voice (Buz's brother) answered from inside, and the guys grumbled and left.

If your gut is telling you to listen up, don't ignore it. *Do not make assumptions about other people, especially those based on stereotypes,* but when someone cues you, don't try so hard not to be racist or some other not-PC thing that you get stupid.

Years later, I fully processed this experience.

And now I can say: Use your discernment, always and with everyone.

Stupid is as stupid does, and you might not live to talk about it.

Glad *I* did.

5
WHAT'S YOUR STORY?

So now I've told you some of my story. What's *yours*?

My parents were survivors, I'm a survivor, and you're a survivor. We are all survivors of what we have gone through, or we wouldn't be here. My mother survived the murder of her entire immediate family and the untimely death of her husband, let alone the move to a foreign country; my father survived the murder of most of his family and the loss of his professional prestige; and I survived the two of them, abandonment, rape, and a pile of other things.

Some of us have had an easier time than others. But whatever you have been through, I hope you won't define yourself by it.

Whatever happened to you *is just your story*. It's **not you**.

I learned that from Joy, but it took me many years to understand what she meant by our "stories"—and, until I did, I was annoyed at her, and hurt, because I felt she didn't understand. Now I get it, and it gets to the heart of what I am trying to say here.

The more you stick to your story, the more it will stick to you. It isn't you, but it will become you—or, rather, you will become it.

For example, another part of my story is being molested as a child, nearly raped as a teen, and raped as an adult. I still have residual fears. But I found that thinking of myself in relation to those men, and what they did, consumed ever more of my space and energy. It was exhausting.

The more you stick to a story of harm, the more it will stick to you—and the more you will actually be harmed. The more you feel like a victim, the more you will be(come) or remain one.

The more you hang onto a victim identity, the more it will come back to you as reality.

The enslavement of Black folks in our country and the racism and discrimination they continue to face daily is a key part of U.S. history—a key part of the story of the U.S. and of Black people. But it is not who Black people are. It is a fact, but it also becomes a story. Part of the same story as slavery. Part of the story of being Black. Part of a story that a Black child does not know until they are told it.

I don't know what Native Americans do, but all of my Black friends and their parents have struggled with what to tell their children, and how and when, so that they know about their origins and what they face, so they are proud, so they don't grow big chips on their shoulders and feel like victims. I have indescribable respect for them and that challenge, and am always very moved and impressed by what my friend Marita Rivero—whom I have known since I was a year old—said about how her parents raised her and her brother (excerpted here from my interview with her for *Different: Our Universal Longing for Community*, which is set in Lincoln University):

*I think my parents were busy using opportunities to explain race to their children in ways that would not deflate and defeat us. I remember asking my mother, "But **why** don't White people like us? Why? Why?" I can still hear the frustration in her voice when she finally said, "Because, Marita, the White man is preposterous!" [Laughs] I said, "Oh, OK." So, if they didn't like me, it was on them—it had nothing to do with me. They were preposterous—that was terrific! [Laughs] I also remember my mother explaining that our people came from Africa. She didn't explain slavery, just that we were rooted somewhere.*

My brother Juan was kind of a hanger-on listening to all of this, and I think he was five or six, so I would have been nine or ten. And he piped up with, "So Marita's an African?" My mother said yes. Well, Juan went into wild laughter and ran out of the house to tell everyone on the campus: "Marita's an African! Marita's an African! Because when we grew up, Lincoln [University] had a high percentage of African students, and they seemed different from us—they were Africans, and we were not. So Juan thought it was screamingly funny that I, who thought I was so clever, was an African! [Cracks up] ...

[One day] the doorbell was ringing, and I said, "There's a White man on the porch." Daddy got up, annoyed, and said, "That's not a White man—that's a man." And I said to my mother, "What's he talking about? It is too a White man!" [Laughs] And she said, "Well, Marita, you know those pictures of little pickaninnies in books who are bug-eyed? 'There's a White man on the porch!' Your father does not have that view of the world." And I guess he was disappointed that despite everything he's said—about how every man puts his pants on one leg at a time—despite everything he's done, his daughter still tells him that there's a White man on the porch! [Laughs more]

It isn't that we ignored race altogether. When my parents gave parties, they would say, "All the White people are going to show up between 8:00 and 8:15. And the Black people aren't going to come till 8:30 or so, but they'll stay till 10:30 or 11:00, and all the White people will go home at 10:00." [More laughter] My mother was running around, "Oh God, my hair isn't ready, what time is it? You know the Joneses are going to be here at 8:00—who's going to answer the door?" [Laughs] It was that kind of sense that we're different people—we had different mores—and of course, my mother was very clear, politically, about the struggle: "This is what's been going on, and your grandparents," etc., so we knew all about our family and the efforts they'd made to fight segregation, and a lot of history.

But we weren't seen as being oppressed. We were to fight the fight against these people who were so stupid and had power to impose stupid restrictions on us because we were every bit as good as they were. A leadership role was implied there, though we were never told we had to lead anything or do anything, but "you don't have to put up with that." You're an intelligent person, and you weren't supposed to hide from reality, and you were supposed to go on with your life—and that entailed having to take on some of those larger issues. But that was to push back enough for you to be able to live your life the way anybody else can. It's a push to recognize your right as a human being to live your life as fully as you can.

Sometimes, we'd be sitting out in the back yard on a summer night, and we'd just have finished this wonderful meal and friends were over, and my parents were having iced tea or whatever. And my dad would say, "I wonder what the White man's doing today." The implication being: it doesn't get any better than this.

So, I think the idea was that we're going to enjoy our life. We're going to enjoy this life and make it as full as it can possibly be, and we'll fight for that. But we're not going to ruin our whole life feeling, "Uuoo, I wish I were White; ugh. . . I didn't get this . . . ughh . . . I can't do that . . . uug—it's not worth it to get up in the morning because they boxed me in over here and they... that is not how we're going to approach life. (Different: Our Universal Longing for Community, 2016; excerpts from Chapter 13)

Marita became a leading figure in public broadcasting.

6

THE NEW & ONLY APPROVED BULLY

One of the cornerstones of PC is its anti-bullying ethic. *Now, PC has become the new (and the only approved) bully.*

If we question or challenge it, we know that the social and legal penalties can be severe. We will likely be instantly and automatically considered a prejudiced right-winger. We alarm and confuse our friends.

It is far easier to comply than make waves, and people do not generally want to hurt or offend someone, so they simply obey the ever-changing PC rules. But, as I said earlier, PC is robbing us of any chance to have the kind of real (and probably difficult) dialogue that offers any hope for meaningful change. We tread on eggshells around the "good" people in the victim categories, afraid to say anything wrong, but we can call the "bad" people names.

*PC has reversed who is considered trash, but the idea that **any** human being should be considered trash has not been trashed.*

We have simply stood the thing on its head.

We have simply exchanged who's which.

And, through PC, individuals who are considered victims—or belong to a victim category—can become terrible bullies (and some have). PC gives them the right to tell us what we can and cannot ask,

27

can and cannot say, must accept and may not object to. These are rights that no one else has.

You may never go against, or even question, someone in this "category" of human being.

They govern their category.

PC governs your mouth.

But you can say anything about groups and individuals who have historically been and are considered oppressors.

Through PC the bully, the government and *some* victims have become bullies.

In my book, no bully is acceptable, and society must include everyone.

I've been bullied a lot, and I have no tolerance for it. I also allowed it. And the more you do a victim thing—a *poor me* thing—when you are bullied, the more you will be bullied.

I guarantee it because bullies love a victim. Bullies *need* a victim. There is no bullying if there are no victims.

7
WHY PC IS A BOOBY-TRAP

I was in the PC bubble until, in an aha moment, I realized that it's a booby-trap: it looks good from the outside but will harm you. And I still feel displaced, dazed, and lonely. Longtime friends are not making this journey with me. Some think I have gone off the rails. Some think I have no business talking about this.

But I have been trying to get across, in a personal way, that feeling like a victim—or identifying someone else as a victim—is one of the most destructive things for a human being. Not only do you treat people differently if you consider them victims—people who buy into that identity, or form it on their own, *don't go anywhere.* As I noted earlier, they even unconsciously self-sabotage to create a reality that matches their idea of it, so victim status becomes a self-fulfilling prophecy.

I know because I did it.

Therapists know this, too. It's Therapy 101. (A common expression among therapists who work with addicts is: "There are no victims, only volunteers.") But this awareness does not seem to compute or apply when it comes to PC, and I think that this can only be the case because therapists have bought into PC and fail to see that it is victim-based. But the victim thing is what makes *PC worst of all for the very people it is supposed to protect.*

PC is a set of rules about how to behave and what to say so that we don't inadvertently offend someone who is considered a victim or member of a victim category (or a survivor). But it doesn't do anything real to change our difficulty with diversity.

It can't, because it's not communication. It's a form of anti-communication. And this is key.

We are told what we can and cannot say—what we should and must not think. We communicate in knots to make sure that we do not say the wrong thing. We are awkward instead of real. We may even feel guilty or deny our perceptions (as I did) if they go against what we are supposed to think. We obey and live according to carefully crafted and ever-changing rules and regulations that we are not allowed to question. PC has become extreme, and many people are chafing under its yoke.

I don't see how it can *ever* be good for citizens not to question government and policy. Not if we want freedom, not if we want a thinking citizenry. Not if we want a democracy.

Nor do I think that automatic acceptance and blind obedience indicate real respect or caring, even when practiced by people who mean well. We are not treating people as equals when we let them dictate without question. *Poor them*, they have been oppressed (truthfully so), so they get to dictate the playing field and the saying field without question. This is not a society I want—*any more than I wanted it the way it was before PC.* This is not equality. (And this is not about Trump: he's the understandable, ready-at-hand, but easy way out of a deeper conversation that many people don't want to have, or don't think we need to.)

Joy once said, "Love is the energy that comes directly from our integrity—from who we really are." I was taken aback by that. I had never heard such a definition of love, and I never forgot it.

PC does not come from the self or from real love. It fundamentally involves compliance.

When we have been deeply hurt, it requires courage and intention and self-love and joy and the intent to let it go and to identify in a way that benefits us. It requires work and often requires help. PC cheats us of that opportunity because it sets us on a never-ending quest to preserve and protect a victim status and to make sure that everyone else does that, too. We may feel acknowledged for our pain, and I know from personal experience how important that is, but we will also stay angry and unfulfilled.

PC is not about love or understanding. It is about guilt and victims. It is based on the idea that categorizing oppressed people as victims is good for them. That's certainly understandable, and it's always easier to identify as a victim, but it is destructive to the core and is always harder on us in the long haul.

It is never fulfilling to feel like a victim, and it is addictive. Even identifying as a survivor, which tries to address the negativity of a victim status, circumscribes how we are thought of and how we think of ourselves: we still identify according to something we have endured.

I acknowledge and deeply honor survivors—I am one myself—and I am keenly aware that severe trauma changes us. But all of us are so much more than anything we go through, even unimaginable horrors. What happened to you is not who you are.

Many of the world's people suffer atrocities so unspeakable that it is difficult for us to grasp them. It is *only **because** of the suffering in this world that there is a need to address the victim thing.*

When I was growing up, people did not want to be considered a victim. That might have been partly because we tended to blame the victim. But it was also before PC made victim identity a coveted status, a badge of honor. *Being a victim has become the prized currency of our time.* People exert themselves to be considered a victim, partly because entitlements come with it, but also because of the social status it brings. People want to be thought of as valuable (people *are* valuable), and victims of any kind are especially valued. We love and esteem our victims in a way that cannot be acquired any other way in our culture. These days, being a victim has become the best thing you can be.

I think that's why the victim identity has become so pervasive.

Affirmative action, possible reparations, and other policies are meant to redress longstanding social inequities and level the playing field, but we can do those things without identifying those individuals as victims—and it's essential that we do not. I am not quibbling over a word. We can recognize and rectify inequity without taking the *poor you* step. We can make things right without falling into that booby-trap.

Is victim status the way we want to identify ourselves and each other? Is that the measure we want to take of each other? Does it describe who we are? It seems that we are now either a member of an oppressed category (a victim, a good guy) or an oppressor (a bad guy).

The difference between acknowledging and appreciating what has happened to someone and defining them as a victim is the difference between hope and hopelessness; between strength and weakness; between an active, soulful connection and abject, passive pity.

Is there any hope of forming a genuine appreciation for others—at least some genuine respect—not just toeing a line and tiptoeing around? I am not saying anything new. I am just saying it again, and from a somewhat different perspective.

PC is costing us so much that I cannot sit by. My conscience requires me to speak up.

Joy recently said, "We are losing our dignity."

I hadn't thought of it that way.

But it's true.

8
READY TO BE OFFENDED

Many of us are just waiting to be offended. Others are walking on eggshells, scared to speak.

Why?

For one thing, intentions do not count anymore.

They are not PC.

I know, I know: the road to hell is paved with good intentions. But if good intentions are irrelevant when someone lacks understanding and information, how can things get better? You can bark at them and shut them up and shut them down, as PC does, and they will comply, but they won't understand or appreciate where you are coming from, which could promote real change. They will never get to know you, and you will never get to know them.

If you have been or are oppressed, it's not your job to educate someone else. It is grotesque to ask that. But how *will* we change? How will people learn who need and seek education, but don't know how to go about it? It's a real question.

A Black Uber driver told me that White people often ask her for the Black perspective on something. She was sick of it. If you are White, do you understand why that question bothers her? Answer: you would never ask a White person that because you know there is no such thing as a White perspective; you are simply speaking to an individual. The people who ask the Uber driver that question are racist, exhausting, and infuriating. But they don't know better, they mean well, and they are trying to learn about Black folks because *the powers that be* have made very sure that we live separately and barely know each other.

I get it. I recently tried to work on racism with a well-intentioned all-White church congregation, and the members were so naïve that I had to walk away. I just couldn't do it. Had they been living under a rock?

But what are we going to do about it?

Unless we want to continue that way (and you might), I think we will have to take intention into account. Some kinda way.

White folks are always saying racist things without intending to. Now they tread on eggshells. Men say sexist things, often without intending to. Some of them now tread on eggshells. Straight people say offensive things to gays. Some of them are walking on eggshells (or just not talking).

Eggshells make for a highly unstable foundation—very bad flooring. Ever noticed that?

If not, try walking on them.

While some people intend to be nasty to others, I am speaking of the many who mean well and don't know what to do. As I've said, you can put people in their places, and they will learn not to say or do certain things.

But where does it leave us?

When you shut someone up and shut someone down, what have you done to warrant their respect? And what have you accomplished? They will probably fear and resent you. They will behave differently in the future. And if that's all you want, you got it. But that's probably all you'll get. They will treat you with the appearance of respect you want, but that doesn't mean they respect you. Maybe you don't care if they do. Maybe the appearance of respect is all you want or believe you can hope for. That would be understandable and far easier.

But we cannot move things forward that way. We are at an impasse.

And how do you feel when someone does that to you?

Have you ever naively said something that offended someone? That's what PC is intended to avoid. I get it. I don't want to hurt anyone. But PC has very harmful, unintended consequences and transforms ignorant mistakes into villainous, unforgivable behavior. It makes people bad and wrong.

We need to choose whether we want to move forward in (justifiable) anger—or come, as Martin Luther King, Jr. did, from a willingness to try to understand, forgive, and teach.

In other words, try to stop coming from our entrenched, automatic, PC-based readiness to be offended.

Life will be lighter. I promise.

9
OH NO YOU DON'T!

The rush-hour subway in New York City is no place to be if you can be someplace else: it's rough, it's rude, it has too many people in too little space and trains that constantly break down. It's an overwhelming environment, and everyone is angry. Most stay glued to their phones. But everyone knows that the human situation is volatile and can explode in a flash. Heads down, no eye contact—the only way to survive.

And there I was, at seventy-three, on a cane after a foot injury (and feeling very much like a victim), being racially bullied almost every day. Sometimes it was subtle; sometimes it was overt.

One morning, for example, I happily slid into a vacant seat in the section of the subway car that is legally designated as priority seating for the elderly and people with disabilities. It was rare to find an empty seat on a rush-hour train. *Ahhh*, I thought, for a blissful split-second. Then a Black woman across the car, staring at me hatefully, began shouting to her companion, loudly enough for at least half the car to hear: "These people with disabilities just think they can run over everybody. Give 'em an inch and they take a mile! They think they're in charge of the world." She raged on, glaring at me and baiting me.

Now, if you know what's good for you, you'd better not *ever* get up in a Black person's conversation with someone else. I knew that, but I was pissed, and therefore stupid. I took the bait. *Balls to the wall*, I thought, and said to her, "I'm seventy-three and on a cane. You got a problem with that?" (Really, Corinna?! You know better than to mess with Black women! They have been messed with *all their lives* and are masters at putting people in their place. And talk about a pathetic, *classic* victim response—OMG! I need a mortified emoji here.)

She lashed out: "My mother is eighty-four and she still stands up on the train! And shut up, I'm not talking to you!" On and on and on, while her (Black) companion just sat quietly and looked uncomfortable.

Hold up. *Please* understand that most Black and other individuals, White and of color (including many young Black men, some of whom were dressed "street," in a way that some Whites fear) graciously and promptly offered me their seat on the train. I am *not* badmouthing Black folks. They were simply my teachers in this case because of my personal history. And I noticed that, when I got a victim vibe from *anyone*, they didn't get up for me (and some people just don't care). *Being kind to others is hard when you feel like a victim, and you assume they are not.*

Of course, the woman who went off on me was not reacting to something I had done, because I hadn't done anything to her or to anyone else. She was blasting me for being White and privileged, and she wanted an audience for her tirade. I understood that before I opened my big defensive mouth.

I was born White—I cannot change that. I went to jail, marched, organized, risked my life, and spent years trying to help end racial injustice in this country. If you don't know me, and I didn't do anything to you (or anyone else), do not make assumptions about me, just because I am White, and I will not make assumptions about you, just because you are Black (or anything else).

I am grateful to that woman and the others who bullied me on the subway for helping me to change my life. It got so extreme that I finally made a subconscious internal decision that I wasn't having it.

And a couple of weeks later, I realized that it had stopped—totally stopped!

I was *amazed*!

I did not get racially bullied on the subway anymore.

I had finally gotten my boundary straight. No more internal guilt for my unchangeably White existence.

And it translated—without a word or any evident change in me!

Apparently, I was putting out a different vibe. I was not that victim, and I was not going to be that victim. It wasn't good for me *or* for the bully. I was done.

As Dave Chappelle said: "I'm Black, but I'm also Dave Chappelle."

Yeah. And I'm White, but I'm also Corinna Fales.

10
GRATITUDE & BOUNDARIES

Letting go of a victim identity can be very difficult. And you will need gratitude and boundaries to do it. They are forms of love.

GRATITUDE

When we feel like a victim, we focus on the bad stuff in our lives, which grows our feeling of being a victim. Keeping our attention and energy on what hurts (or has hurt) us interferes with attracting better things, people, and positivity into our lives.

That's not a judgment or a canned philosophy. It's an observation.

I am not a rah-rah type of person, and this is not a commercial for gratitude. Also, there is a difference between positivity and gratitude. Positivity is an attitude with which we approach life. It is a powerful agent for change, and a good thing. But positivity has also been commercialized and become big business. I am speaking of humble, pure gratitude—simply being thankful. Not because it will get us something.

For years, I have noticed that I not only feel better when I remember to be grateful (e.g., for breathing normally, for legs that work, for the roof over my head, for the beautiful day), I am also frequently surprised by good things that suddenly show up, seemingly out of nowhere. When you feel like a victim, you're always angry and nothing is good enough.

The more grateful I am, the more good things seem to come my way. It's not an abstract principle to me that we get back what we manifest in our lives.

Gratitude is key to a sense of well-being and how we receive life and process our experiences. And to what we bring into our lives.

And it will likely be tested often.

> "Our attitudes control our lives. Attitudes are a secret power working twenty-four hours a day for good or bad. It is of paramount importance that we know how to harness and control this great force."
>
> – Irving Berlin
>
> https://www.brainyquote.com/quotes/irving_berlin_119768 - accessed on 10.24.19

BOUNDARIES

Boundaries are fundamental to what makes us who we are. They define where we begin and end, the space in which we exist. Every entity has to have them. Boundaries define an entity, plain and simple.

If you don't have good boundaries, you will feel like a victim because you will become one. People know when they can walk all over you.

The stronger your boundaries, the less likely you are to feel like a victim. Although discrimination occurs that has nothing to do with your boundaries, *how you process it, does.*

The boundary business has been a lifelong work for me, and I am still engaged in it. When I set and maintain clear boundaries—and, with that, become a more grateful human being—I don't feel like a victim. It is *that* essential to the victim issue. Likewise, someone who does not feel like a victim is able to set good boundaries (but is not just waiting to be offended).

Because my mother did not regard me as a separate human

being—physically, mentally, emotionally, or spiritually—she violated every boundary I tried to establish and punished me for having the nerve to try. (I often think that the deepest divide in the world is between people who got the love they needed as children, and those who did not; there are profound and readily apparent differences between them.)

For years, I worked with Joy and Bob to locate and set some boundaries. What should they be, and where did they belong? It was a *huge* mystery to me—I puzzled over it endlessly and obsessively—until I finally realized that I only need one boundary: self-love and self-respect, my integrity as a human being. To this day, I could care less about many boundaries that other people (who are more proper than I am) care about. But if you do not respect my integrity or *try* to hurt me, I have learned who you are. And *what* you are does not matter to me *at all*.

These days, many people are poised to be offended. *When you feel like a victim, you are just waiting to be offended. Taking offense has become a modern form of self-love and respect in our PC world.*

But part of **real** self-love is **not** being offended by every little thing. I am not saying to let people disrespect you—ever. It's just that the more you *truly* love yourself and know who you are, the less gets under your skin.

You'll just know that they're preposterous.

11
AYO

It is a great privilege to have met Ayo and been able to interview her. [I have changed her name and identifying details of her story.] Given her formidable background, it would have been a shoo-in for her to become a statistic and be a poster child for victims. But this interview reveals why she has risen to the top. Let her inspire you. She began:

When you look at where I started—making $29,000, to being an HR director making $95,000, to being an executive director of administration making six figures—there was no formal education training, there was just people investing in me, me being willing to dedicate myself, and me reflecting the generosity of the people around me. That's all it was. People always ask me why I'm so happy and bubbly. First, it costs too much to be miserable. Second, I have amazing people around me, a job I love, a healthy family. I can pay my bills and have gone further than I could have imagined, especially considering where I came from. There are things I could worry about, but they never outweigh what I have.

Let's talk about where you came from...

I had a grandmother, God rest her soul, who had ten children. She was poor, uneducated, and married to an abusive husband. Of her first eight children, which she had during the '50s when there were no family planning options, the youngest was my biological mother. Abortion wasn't legal, there were restrictions on what women could own in terms of property, in terms of having economic independence. I didn't know this. I didn't see how it impacted and shaped her life. But I understand it now.

This woman went from her father's house to her husband's house. She was a baby-making machine, and she was miserable. She tried to commit suicide several times. The last time, one of her youngest sons found her unconscious on the floor, with pills and alcohol. And I guess because of the trauma it caused him, she promised herself she'd never do it again.

So, when I came along, she was very different from the woman who did all those things. Of her three boys and five girls, all five girls, to my knowledge—and not everyone knows this—were molested by her husband, their father. She went to court to fight for her kids and attest to the type of man her husband was, but he owned property and the judge saw fit for him to take care of the children because he had the financial means. And not only did the judge *not* protect my grandmother or her children from this man—he gave him full custody. So, eventually, her children were taken away. I could tell it was extremely painful for her.

She moved, left her girls behind, and ended up marrying a guy who helped take care of her when her husband was out gambling the money away. She had two children with this second man, only to find out that he was also abusive, but not as bad. He didn't abuse his own children.

Now, there were ten kids. My mother was the youngest child from my grandfather. And she had a drug problem. I believe heroin was her drug of choice. She had her first child at sixteen. Her second child, who would have been my older brother, died. And, after he died, she was deemed unfit to take care of her children, and her first child (my oldest sister) was taken away by her paternal grandparents. But my mother kept getting pregnant. She had me, my brother, my sister. And three more.

All these children were by different men. During the four years I lived with her, I acquired two siblings. Me, my sister, and my brothers are all from different fathers.

She was physically abusive to my younger brother and my sister. She was always high, but we didn't know because we were so young. She was just angry all the time, and she would leave for days. We lived in a shelter, and I remember cockroaches attacking us. She would put a pot out—like a box of macaroni and cheese—and leave. And because we had no idea when she was coming back, we would run back and forth into the pot and grab macaroni out and eat it. We sometimes did that for days.

How old were you at this point?

I was four. My brother was three, and my sister was one. I remember trying to make pancakes, and the middle was still liquid. We'd watch MC Hammer videos in front of the box TV on the floor and eat liquid pancakes. But we were fine while she was away, because everything we did when she was there would make her angry. We didn't understand what was going on.

A four-year-old, a three-year-old, and a one-year-old took care of yourselves...

Yes. And my three-year-old brother was severely asthmatic, to the point that he had a machine, and I was the only one who knew how to use it. There were several times when he almost died, between the abuse and the negligence. So I was very protective of him.

The State awarded my grandmother custody of us after seeing the physical abuse we went through. So we moved in with her [into a very rough neighborhood], and she was mean—really mean. I'd be mean, too, if somebody pumped me fulla babies, and I went through everything that she went through. We stayed there a year or two, but I guess she was too old to deal with us, so then we moved in with my aunt—my mother's oldest sister. By the time we moved to her place, I was about six.

I was raised by her, and I call her my mother. The difference in age between her and my biological mother was so great that my aunt's children were old enough to raise us. This woman, very strong, not educated at all, grew up in poverty. Her mother had had to collect cans and bottles to feed them when my grandfather was out gambling his money away.

Living with her, my family became very well known for violence, for fighting, for being like a little gang with the same last name. But very protective. You're taught to protect each other. You're taught to know how to survive. You're taught to be tough.

Now we're in [one of the roughest neighborhoods in the country]. And, mind you, my aunt already has four children. By nineteen, she was married with four children. She was married twenty years to an abusive husband who beat the crap out of her. Military, just like my grandfather. He eventually died of AIDS.

By the time my aunt got custody of us, she was a single woman with a household. We got fed, and we had clean clothes. People were angry and miserable, but we were not neglected.

My brother had a behavior problem, and my sister had a big mouth. I was the quiet one who always wanted to be alone. I loved reading and writing because they were an escape for me. My paper didn't tell anyone my secrets, so I could get my feelings out, and reading was a vacation, a trip to fantasyland. I spent hours by myself because I never felt comfortable around my family. They were hostile and aggressive in a way that was not natural to me.

As I got older, I remember angry rants: "You're gonna be like your mother!" That was my aunt's daughter talking; she was older, like seventeen, so she watched us when my aunt worked. She would hit us, she would yell at us, she would curse at us. We were like little child laborers. But what she did in that child bootcamp, which I appreciate to this day, is that we learned how to clean house, to cook, to do our laundry—all by the time I was seven. And I was the oldest of the three. We were very self-sufficient. But she was very hard on us.

I was academically inclined. I grasped concepts easily. But I was always distracted and never did my homework. Those were my problems, but my teachers always loved me. And I was a protective person, except when it came to myself. If you did anything to my two siblings, that shy person went out the door and somebody else came through. But outside of that, I was very non-confrontational, very closed off. It came from being kind of timid and seeing the aggressiveness around me and thinking, "Let's not poke the bear."

We were told several times—when we were verbally or physically abused and attempted to complain or tell anybody—that no one was kicking down any doors to come save us. Like, basically, your mother and your father didn't think enough of you to show up. So you can just suck it up.

It made us all tough in a way. I don't know if it's a good way. My brother has been in and out of jail for the last ten years, usually for fights, drugs, weapons. He goes in for a few years, comes out, does something else and goes back in. My sister is doing pretty well. She and I are very close. She looks up to me, relies on me. She's very disciplined. She [has a good job] and she's in college, working towards her first degree.

Back to our childhood, the abuse there was mostly verbal. The physical abuse wasn't extreme, especially compared to my biological mother, and we had social workers, so you couldn't leave marks. But there was a lot of verbal and mental abuse—a lot of belittling.

In our family, it was like we were inferior in some way. We were the bottom of the barrel of grandchildren or cousins. No one was below us. My mother was the bottom, so we were the bottom.

We grew up—went to junior high, high school. I think socially I survived. I like to be by myself, but I'm very social. I think it began as a survival technique because you cannot live in a ghetto by yourself. My brother got beat up because he wouldn't join a gang. You couldn't go to school and live on our block and not be part of us. You had to establish yourself on a social level or they would chew you up and spit you out. I also made it a big deal to establish myself as a respected individual because I didn't feel that we were respected, growing up. Respect and image were a big deal for me. Not only did my siblings look up to me—people were looking at me. My image mattered.

That saved me from making a lot of mistakes—like drug use, being promiscuous, having a baby, because I wasn't about to look like an idiot. Nobody was going to make a fool of me. I understood that if I got pregnant, I would be homeless. My aunt made that clear to me when I was twelve, and I believed her. I understood the real-life consequences at a very early age. I was literally gonna be on the streets, and then what?

Things like that kept me out of trouble. And then there were beatings associated with trouble. I got hit maybe twice by my aunt, and

I couldn't take it. I was very strategic about the things I did; I was very good at determining what consequences I could and couldn't handle. And it kept me out of trouble.

I was failing in school, and no one knew. I was alcoholic, and no one knew. And all of this was when I was fifteen. I used to sleep with liquor under my pillow. My house was the center of the family, and it was the party house; liquor and drugs were always available. The adults were into their own thing and didn't pay us any mind, and we were so well trained that they didn't have to think about us. If my aunt yelled at you, and you looked at her wrong, boy, you were waking up from the twilight in about five seconds! You had to make your facial expressions appropriate. Forget talking back. That didn't even cross your mind. You were too busy worrying if you *looked* confrontational. There were just certain things we wouldn't do. We didn't run away, we knew the right things to tell the social workers and the therapists, we didn't talk back. We were very well-behaved and easy-to-deal-with kids. If my aunt *ever* found out that you spoke to an adult in an inappropriate manner, you would not need your dental plan anymore. That was crystal clear!

Do you think it was a good thing?

I think it was a good thing to a degree. I think it built the humbleness I have, and a certain level of respect and appreciation for people, which carried me forward. I tell my son, "If you're not respectful and mindful in how you interact with people, no one wants to be around you." I never felt like an outcast outside of my family. I think that helped me. I think it opened doors. I'm a very approachable person and a pretty mindful person, though it's wearing off as I get older. [Laughter]. I'm very aware of how my words and actions impact other people. It helps me, even when I speak about work and how employees are affected by the way they are treated. I was promoted to supervisor just two years into my regular entry-level job. No warning, no application, nothing. But I was already a team leader. People already came to me for answers, so there was no issue with the transition. It came naturally to me because I worked *with* people, not *over* people. That was just how I was naturally inclined to interact with people, no matter what their positions or titles were. And I understand how important team is.

Do you think there's an inborn something in you, or that it was conditioned, or a combination...?

I think it might be a combination. Who knows? We were all raised in the same household with the same conditions, and we are not the same people, especially when it comes to that. My sister is doing well, but she's outspoken in a way that I'm not. I'm candid and straightforward, but she's outspoken in a way that dismisses other people's feelings. And my brother is on another level. So, maybe some part of it is innate, but I think part of it was also triggered—or was switched on—by conditioning and our environment. Respect and appreciation were reinforced. It was always thrown in our faces what people did for us. We knew the value and the price of everything we had because people reminded us of every sacrifice that they made for us. And I remember one of my mother's [my aunt's] favorite sayings: "This world owes you nothing." I must have made that part of my DNA because it's how I function on every level.

...Which gets to the heart of what I'm looking at in this book because I'm writing a lot about why one person goes down in that situation, which would be the easier thing to do, and why you didn't. And I wonder whether part of it is this kind of attitude? Did you feel like a victim as a child? Did you get over it?

I felt hurt, really hurt, and angry. In a way that I couldn't express. That's where the writing came in. My diary was where I could express my anger. I was still hurt and angry often, but I would never feel sorry for myself. Because the truth is, even though it was thrown in our faces in a way that I would never do as an adult, it *was* the truth. The truth is, we could have had it worse. The alternative to people saying bad words and making you feel bad, is your mother killing you. We were alive, we were healthy, our clothes were clean, and we had more food than we could eat.

We were very grateful. It could have been a lot worse. Yes, they guilt-tripped us all the time, but it's one thing to understand their intent and another thing to understand my perception of it. Whatever their intent was, I understood that those were facts. Whatever their incentive was to remind me of those facts, it was still true. We lived in a hood, so, in addition to what went on in our own family, we were surrounded by kids whose parents were drug addicts, prostitutes, whose fathers were convicts, murderers, drug dealers. These kids were abandoned, too. Just because their parents were physically in the house, or one parent was physically in the house, doesn't mean that their situation wasn't as bad as ours. My aunt would drink a six-pack every night, but she didn't snort cocaine and shoot up heroin.

When I think about the things I was exposed to and compare them to what I could have been exposed to, considering the neighborhood, it could always be worse, much worse. What I *hadn't* seen until I got older, was that things could be better. My life was good until I got to high school and figured out it wasn't. It was like: I got saved from a homicidal mother, and I have a family who doesn't starve me, doesn't rape me, and doesn't beat me (to the point where I can't walk or I'm physically impaired). So yeah, it could be worse. But I failed to realize that it could be better. Now I know that I was depressed, but then I just thought I was tired, all the time, mentally and physically. And, for a *little* while, I contemplated killing myself. But suicides go to hell. Kill somebody else: God will forgive you. I figured that out when I was eleven or twelve. [Laughter]

As a coping mechanism, laughter works. It helps put things into perspective. It keeps me from taking myself too seriously.

I don't have the feeling with you that it's just a defense mechanism…

Yes, it is genuine. But it also saves me. I've *seen* misery. I *grew up* with misery. That's why I tell people, "Your misery *can't* impact me. I just won't allow it." The one thing I take from my childhood and always tell people is that [nothing] could send me back to my childhood, for one reason: As a child, you have no control over your environment, the people in your life, your circumstances. Everything about your life is at somebody else's will. That was the hardest thing about childhood. There was nothing I could do about it.

And I promised myself that when I became an adult, *nobody* would *ever* put me in this position. That contributed to my independence, my crippling independence! I'm getting better now, at thirty-three. But I just felt that giving people blame meant giving them power. Blaming people for your problems, for anything wrong, gives them *power*. And I *refused* to do that. I promised myself as a child that nobody would ever have this power over me, once I change this. And that's another really strong principle that I live by. If anything is wrong or right, it's my fault.

Where did you get that from?

I think maybe it's a derivative of "the world owes you nothing." Because you want to cry. You want to say, "Woe is me." You want to say, "How come I don't have the mother that does x,y,z?" Or "Why do people treat me mean and bad?" What do you mean?! This world don't owe you a damn thing. You think that someone's supposed to be nice to you—*supposed* to *give* you something?

Anything that you want, figure out how you're gonna get it. It's nobody else's responsibility, including your family's.

So, there was no victim mentality in the house. Period. Right?

None. And it was so strong that I despise victims. That sounds bad, but it's one thing when I advocate for a group of oppressed people—it's another thing for me to communicate with them individually. I can't do it. I struggle to sympathize with people. I can do it in a PC manner, but when I do, it's not necessarily genuine because it's not how I see the situation. To some degree, if I tell you I sympathize with your struggles, I'm lying to you, because I don't. I'm like, "Suck it up." But you can't say that to people. Everyone can't suck it up. My brother and sister showed me that. I would say, "We've established that you've been abused, that you weren't treated right, that your daddy didn't show up, that your momma don't care. Fill up a pamphlet with all the things done wrong to you. What are you going to do about it? Because nobody cares. You remember: 'Nobody's kicking down any doors to save you.' So, what are *you* going to do? Because if you're going to stay there, you might as well get used to it and learn to like it. If you don't like it that much, fix it. We're not children anymore. The one thing we have is the ability to change our lives."

And once I got this power, I was power hungry! To this day, I have not seen my mother since my son was born, which is over a year. I have not seen the rest of my family, except for my sister and brother, in at least two years.

[A specific event triggered that:] I was raped. I was to be the bridesmaid in a wedding for my, quote, cousin's. And, long story short, her fiancé raped me. When I drink a lot, I go to sleep and sleep like a log. My cousin brought me home to her apartment and laid me on the couch. She said I was passed out. Disoriented, I woke up later with her fiancé, who had been at work, on top of me. He raped me in their house while she was in the next room.

Initially, my reaction was not to tell her. The problem with rape is not just the person who did it—it's everybody else it impacts. And as my cousin drove me home in the morning, I was trying to fix this in my mind while she went on and on about her wedding. When something like that happens to you, being a strong woman works against you because you question yourself. How did I let this happen? Why did he think it was OK to do this to *me*?

I immediately dropped out of her wedding. We were buying bridesmaids' dresses and I offered to pay for any expenses she had incurred on my account. She didn't respond to me, and I eventually learned that she thought I wouldn't be in her wedding because I didn't want to pay for my bridesmaid dress!

In that moment, I lost my shit. Motherfuck you! Fuck you and your fat rapist that you're about to marry. And if you want to know why I'm not in your fucking wedding, you can ask your sorry son-of-a-bitch-of-a-man. And I pray you don't have a daughter.

That must have thrown her for a loop because she went hysterical—not to me, but with everybody else, who called me off the hook. Her fiancé had told her we had an affair, and said he was sorry. She hadn't even heard my side. And at that point, I was not even interested in playing sides. Fuck you. All y'all can be outta my life. I like my friends—I chose them. But my uncle [whose goddaughter this was] comes into my life and brings you motherfuckers, and this is what I get. So all ya'll can pack your shit and leave my life.

That was the beginning of my disconnect from my family. My uncle called me and says, "What happened?" And I said, "I feel really bad because I never would have told her. It would have been my problem, and she could have lived her happily-ever-after, and if she found out

...ut on her own. But she ...e said he believed Ayo's ...d to socialize with the ...nip.]

...media and my sister, because s... ...te with. And I know it sounds bad, bu... ...at was the proverbial straw that broke the came... ...e, I felt unprotected. Unvalued. Insignificant. And then I ... and put all those thoughts to the back because I could understand you were all coming from your own insecurities, your own struggles. As a child, I thought you just didn't like me. As an adult, I knew better. You were dealing with your own demons, and what you showed me and did to me was only a reflection of how you felt about yourself. So I knew not to take it personally. But this incident brought it back. My family never had my back. And I would spend hundreds for food and alcohol so everybody could have a good time.

It costs you nothing for me to be in your life. And it cost me everything. So fuck y'all. That's how I feel, from the bottom of my heart. People who don't know the whole story say, "You gotta see your mother; you'll regret it one day." And I'm like, "No, I don't think so."

The beautiful thing is that my family taught me that you can make your own family and probably do a better job. I have people like [her best friend, other friends], my first son's father and his entire family; his mother is like my mother and is there for me in a way that nobody in my family has *ever* been there for me.

It's sad, and it's good. Sad because that's a real fucked-up family. But when you have someone who is a bigger support to you than your entire family combined, that's good, because I *don't* need you. I *don't*. You made me think so, as a child, but I know better as an adult. My family tells me this is ridiculous, and I tell them, "I've never had anybody in my life put me through what my family has put me through. And I've never received the support that I've received from everybody else. So, I don't know what that equivalent of a four-letter word is to you, but it means nothing to me in terms of bloodlines." This is what I told my mother the last time I spoke to her about family. I said people will *not* disrespect me because we share the same last name, or the same bloodline. *That will not happen.*

I don't speak ill of them. They still reach out to me—with no response. People push. But I can sleep at night, knowing that I did nothing wrong to *any* of you. When you tell the story, I want you to tell the whole story, or tell pieces. But in no version of this story do you get to be the victim. You taught me that.

I can't see how it benefits people to feel like a victim. You want to feel hurt? You want to feel pain? You want to feel like you're at the mercy of other people? Who wants that? No, thank you. No. Let's think about options. I can't do miserable people. If you want to be miserable, you need to understand that it's your choice.

I feel lucky, because what most cripples people is not what happens to them, but how they respond to it. And what carries me and motivates me and gives me confidence is, what's the worst that could happen? I can always build myself back up from whatever I lose as a gamble—like taking a risk to go for a position that seems out of my league—or going for anything that seems out of my league. It's like, "Are you good enough for this?" Well, fuck it. If I'm not, we'll find out, won't we? Let somebody show me I'm not good enough. Let's not assume I'm not good enough. Let me find out the hard way.

It's weird, because the person I am as I approach a situation naturally is the opposite of the person I become when I'm in defense mode. Both the fathers of my children will tell you that the easiest way to get me to do something is to tell me I can't do it. If I come up with something and then push myself to do it, it's like, "Ehhhh, I don't know if I'm good enough." But if you tell me I *can't* do it, *"You talkin' to me?! Try me!"*

It's what drives me. And the most difficult thing in my life is that I have run out of people to tell me what I can't do! I gotta find a new motivator! Nobody's telling me what I can't do! I have an alter ego that's like a switch. Something goes off and it's, "Who better than me?" What do you mean, I can't have this? The hell with you!" And I know that part of it is that all my life, people have been telling me what I'm not worth. And all my life, I've been hell-bent on making fools out of all of them.

12

ONLY ONE KIND OF PIZZA?

Some people are super talented at feeling like a victim. A doctor I know refers to them as professional victims.

It would be hard to beat Claudia on that score.

At work one day, the supervisors decided to thank us for our hard work by ordering pizza for everyone and throwing us a party in one of the conference rooms.

But Claudia couldn't leave her post in Reception, so her supervisor asked me to take her a slice. It made me happy to! When I began to hand it to her, however, she made a sad, sour face and asked if it had pepperoni on it. "No," I replied. She sighed, whined, shook her head slowly, and repeated, "No pepperoni? Is there only one kind of pizza?"

"It's free," I said.

She sighed, shook her head and, still shaking her head, finally accepted the slice.

Poor Claudia.

13

TRIGGER WAS A HORSE

When I was growing up, Trigger was a beautiful Palomino horse on a famous TV series. He didn't make anyone cry.

Nowadays, triggers are everywhere, especially on college campuses, and must be avoided because they might upset someone.

Triggers used to be called buttons. They stem from life experiences that hurt us. Nice people tried to avoid pushing someone's buttons if they were aware of them. But buttons were recognized as *belonging to* someone—as coming from someone's personal/social history—not as necessarily or inherently offensive.

Triggers are part of being human and living in this world. How does it help us to transfer all responsibility for the way we deal with our issues onto someone else? How we handle them—and how we grow from that process—now seem to be beside the point. We are just supposed to shut up if we say something that triggers unwanted feelings in someone.

I don't want to hurt or offend anyone. But we cannot grow if we spend our lives trying to avoid pain. In a place (like a workshop) where we need to be vulnerable to grow, it is essential for the space to be safe. In my work with Joy and Bob, I always knew that I was in a totally safe space: I wouldn't be judged, I was loved unconditionally, what I said and did was held in the strictest confidence. I would never have screamed on that mat if I hadn't been sure it was safe for me to do that.

That's what differentiates safe spaces from life, which is not and cannot be safe. How has it become a good thing to avoid—to try to outlaw—everything that hurts? Nowadays, people seem to think that avoidance is the way to deal with anything that makes them feel pain.

Avoidance is not love.

Love does not pretend things that are not so.

Love has integrity.

Love believes that you can deal with life and grow.

That you can work on things that hurt and eventually let them go.

What prepares us for this unsafe world? Makes us grow, develops character and inner strength?

Truth does, reality does, experience does.

We need actuality to grow, and we often grow from hurt. And, since reality is frequently hurtful, we always have opportunities.

> "Just as we develop our physical muscles through overcoming opposition - such as lifting weights - we develop our character muscles by overcoming challenges and adversity."
>
> – Stephen Covey
>
> https://www.brainyquote.com/quotes/stephen_covey_138246 - accessed on 11.21.19

How can we be truly human—with genuine heart and empathy, not some virtual version of that—if we refuse to go where we are touched by something that challenges us to respond in new ways? How does avoidance free us from it? How do we ever let it go when it continues to occupy avoided, unaddressed mental and emotional—even physical—space in our being?

Even children's stories these days are no match for the great fairy tales of old—like Grimm's—which fired our imaginations and hearts by teaching us that we can vanquish our enemies, whether giant or witch or monster. Those beasts are *internal:* they reside in our hearts and the hearts of children. Fairy tales resonate with those internal struggles and reassure children that they can defeat their demons.

Nowadays, though, we have namby-pamby PC stories for children. God forbid there should be a witch, for example: too scary for little children and not PC. Just make sure that the story contains somebody in one of our victim groups and is about being nice to them.

I am always for people being nice and accepting each other, but these stories no longer speak to our greatness of heart and possibility, to colossal courage and grand purpose, to vanquishing dreadful enemies (inside or out). These PC stories would have us flower gently into space, like some carefully tended hothouse plant.

They do not mirror children's hearts. Or ours.

They are soul-less.

No one I know has become greater without pain—certainly not by trying to avoid what pained them. My own growth has been excruciating. And exciting. And interesting. And a constant surprise.

Still is.

Pain inevitably attends life; growing involves letting go of its control over us so we can be free. But the point of PC seems to be to hang onto our pain if it relates to the way we identify—if we are victims.

We will never know who we *really* are if we hang onto what has hurt us. We will just be the thing that keeps us stuck, in place.

In our PC climate, people (at least those who are considered victims) are entitled to shut anyone down who says something they don't want to hear (I am not talking about pejorative name-calling or nastiness). And we seem to think that's right and helpful to everyone.

It isn't.

It's a form of patronizing, and it diminishes.

Accountability is part of therapy and personal growth 101, which have shown us that taking responsibility for ourselves is essential to our development and maturity. Every therapist knows this. And, I repeat, every therapist knows the costs of a victim identity.

Why does it not seem to apply when PC comes into play?

Because PC is not understood to be victim-based.

"Every human has four endowments - self awareness, conscience, independent will and creative imagination. These give us the ultimate human freedom... The power to choose, to respond, to change."

– Stephen Covey

https://www.brainyquote.com/quotes/stephen_covey_138246 - accessed on 11.20.19

14
WHO ARE WE, ANYWAY?

In his famous "I have a dream" speech, Martin Luther King, Jr. hoped that his children would one day be judged by their character, rather than their skin color.

I was at the March on Washington in 1963 when King gave that speech. It was my dream, too, for the nation and for my friends. I had already gone to jail to try to help make that dream a reality—a reality that has not happened. But I did not imagine that I would be watching an LGBTQI sensitivity training video in 2016, in which a young woman proudly describes herself as Latina, single-parent, gender-nonconforming, same-gender loving, queer, and one more thing that I have forgotten. Her description personifies how we want to be known these days, and how we want others to identify us.

This is the time of identity politics.

Now, it seems, we *want* to be judged by the color of our skin and the other identities we claim. The content of our character is virtually irrelevant, like an extinct dinosaur from a bygone age. No one talks about character anymore. What matters now is *what* you are, not *who*.

I could give you my own string of identities, but they will not tell you *who* I am.

While we have been profoundly impacted and shaped by all the categories of human we are, and the experiences we have had in relation to them, we are much more. Those categories do not do us justice.

The attributes listed by the woman in the video are a very important part of her identity and sense of self, as are mine. But do those categories define her or tell you about her character? (To be fair: categories were the subject of that video; perhaps she would have identified herself differently in a different context.)

How she defines herself is obviously her choice, not mine, and if those designations make her feel whole and happy, then I am happy for her. Personally, I would feel like you still didn't know *me*—*who* I am (like Dave Chappelle's: "I am Black, but I am also Dave Chappelle").

My soul is genderless and colorless and ageless. When I connect with it, I have a very different sense of the me that is me than I have when I define myself socially or politically. I feel calm and whole, grounded, and connected to my full potential. My heart may have been broken, maybe many times, but my soul is intact. I am me.

We need to learn about, respect, and honor the *whats* of each other. We need to celebrate our differences, love ourselves, and shine brightly in the world as the individuals and groups we are. But I also want to get to know *who* you are. And I don't want *who you are* to get lost in the crowd of *what* identities.

I hope we will add the content of our character and the deepest, truest parts of ourselves to these political identities. Even replace them. I hope we will include our *who* in our *what*. *I hope we will love and honor ourselves so much that we deeply know ourselves to be far greater than the sum of our hurts or our whats.* And I hope we will remember that everyone is a who, not just a what, and include each other in the human circle without the artifice and authority of PC.

I also hope that we will grasp that *different* is neither worse nor better than *same*. It is simply different.

It used to be considered worse—almost automatically. Now it is considered better—also almost automatically.

I'm just sayin'.

"Once you label me you negate me."

– Søren Kierkegaard

https://www.azquotes.com/author/8000-Soren_Kierkegaard - accessed on 11.20.19

15
PLAYING VICTIM =
PLAYING SAFE

Anytime you play victim, you are playing yourself safe. After all, you can't expect too much of a victim.

In my case, the victim thing still shows up in overeating. I have struggled with my weight all my life. I have lost fifty pounds and gained fifty pounds. I stayed a healthy weight for years and never thought I would let myself get fat again.

But I did.

So, what's up? What am I addicted to?

I was surprised when I realized that overeating expresses my addiction to feeling like a victim.

And I have come to believe that the same thing is true for many overeaters: that weight is where their *poor me* resides. If you ever watch *Catfish* on MTV, you will notice that many "catfishes" are fat and are bitter at being bullied and considered unacceptable as they are. They often use their hurt as an *excuse* to hurt the people they con with false profiles on dating sites. But, like me, they could probably just lose the weight. No more sad sack. It's not easy, but people do it all the time. So why don't they, and why don't I?

As I keep saying, we sabotage ourselves to create and reinforce the reality we need to confirm ourselves as a victim. I got fat again when I felt like a victim again—when I hurt my foot and was on the subway.

If I felt fine about being overweight, it wouldn't have that meaning, but I don't, and it does. (And either way, it isn't good for us.) I am not weight-shaming anyone. Women, especially, tend to struggle with negative self-image and identity issues related specifically to our bodies, and I want to emphasize that individuals who are happy and healthy with their weight probably do not overeat because they identify as victims. (And there is a cultural piece to this that I respect.)

My addiction is to the physical buffer and victim identity that weight seemingly offers. It makes an easy, in-your-face target that protects against potentially deeper hurt. Other issues that people struggle with are often not visible. But fat is just out there, for all to see.

Being fat is a paradox: it makes us both more vulnerable and less vulnerable. It both plays us safe and opens us up to ridicule. When you are fat, you have an immediately apparent vulnerability—and an excuse.

Excuse? For what?

An excuse from expectations of you—from any source.

People expect less from you. You probably expect less of yourself. You don't have to *do* anything. Being a victim is what you do. You play yourself safe. And, ironically, small.

For me, over-eating is self-sabotage. It's not good for me, and it's not funny. But it takes some focus off other things you could hurt me with.

In preparing to release this book, I have been challenged in some very hard ways. Conforming to my mother's expectations of me meant playing life and myself safe, and small. True, jail is not generally known for being a safe space! But the real danger I faced lay in discernibly becoming myself—of stepping into my power, as people say. *That* was the truly unsafe space, the unsafe space I avoided—till now.

While it is obvious now, it came as a revelation to understand how much my fat and the victim ID served me. I had let it go till I found myself being pushed around on the rush-hour subway in New York. Being on that cane I told you about made me feel very old very quickly, and I thought I was stuck with it for the rest of my life. That brought back the victim thing—and, bam—I gained thirty-five pounds.

When I moved to North Carolina, I immediately forgot the cane. Just forgot it. Completely. It was amazing! But I am left with the weight to lose. Now I need to forgive myself, and just do it.

For those of us who struggle with fat, it often becomes our identity. It's not who we are, but it becomes our *story*. Having just remembered, as I write this, how and why I gained weight again, is very helpful. I don't feel stuck in a global story about myself. And that is a huge weight off!

If you struggle with your weight, ask yourself how your weight serves you, because it does. Don't beat yourself up about it. You'll never find out that way and beating yourself up is just more victim behavior. Honor how the fat has served you, thank it for its service, and let it go when you are ready. (You might need to make this decision more than once.)

Terrible, *terrible* things have gone on throughout human time. And it seems they always will. They leave scars, they leave indescribable pain. No one really understands what someone else has been through.

All of us who do the fat victim thing have our reasons, and I love us.

It's terrific that PC makes it wrong to weight-shame people. (In general, it is appalling how much we measure people by appearances.)

If you are super big, you are likely telling us that you are living your life too small, although some have stepped into their power, regardless. But the problem remains that being fat is not healthy. And being a victim isn't either. In trying to be helpful, PC disregards reality.

If I don't lose weight before this book comes out, you will see a fat me. And you will have a ready-made excuse, if you want one, to discount what I say—which would be *you* playing it safe. I am aware that being fat can interfere with my message, and I feel vulnerable writing about it. But I would also feel vulnerable not writing about it. So there I am.

Here, I need to bring up Brené Brown and her wonderful TED Talk, "The Call to Courage," in which she discusses the connection between courage and being vulnerable. Watching it again made me realize that I have been resistant to losing weight for the last year or so because I am getting ready to speak out on PC and will take flak for it. Skinny or fat, however, I am still me, and what I think remains the same. In this case, what I think is that PC's opposition to weight-shaming is great but does not make our fat invisible. Or healthy. Even if we feel fine about it.

Nope, PC just cannot make fat a safe space—for you or for me.

"Our life always expresses the result of our dominant thoughts."

– Søren Kierkegaard

https://www.thefreshquotes.com/soren-kierkegaard-quotes/ - accessed 11.21.19

16
THE PC WOMAN

These days, young Western women are supposed to be free with their bodies—to want and to have casual hookups—to be as emotionally unencumbered about their sexuality as men often are.

If you're a woman and that's your thing, fine. But science shows that women's physiological reaction to sex differs from men's and makes us more emotionally vulnerable.

How un-PC!

But true.

Women produce oxytocin (do not confuse with oxycontin!), a hormone that our brains send to our uterus and breasts to induce labor and let down milk. Commonly referred to as the "love hormone," it is essential to the mother-child bond and to the survival of our species. Moreover, and importantly, sexual activity stimulates the production and release of oxytocin.

While men also produce some oxytocin, studies show that it affects them differently; as of this writing, the jury is still out on the complexities of oxytocin's effects in both sexes and how it interacts with testosterone, vasopressin, and estrogen.[1] It is a fascinating inquiry, which seems to indicate some almost opposite effects in men and in women, but it is not my purpose here to get technical, so you can research it if you want.

[1] Proc Natl Acad Sci U S A. 2016 Jul 5; 113(27): 7650–7654. - accessed on 10/7/19 Published online 2016 Jun 20. doi: [10.1073/pnas.1602620113] PMCID: PMC4941426

My point here is that women and men often respond differently to sexual encounters. It may not be PC to say it, but we talk about it all the time because it comes up all the time.

We are biological beings, and biology is not random. But now we are expected to be biology-free because it does not serve the PC agenda—in this case, a supposedly feminist PC agenda.

I am a feminist.

That means I support women as we are, not as men are (insofar as we are different), and not as some socially constructed version of ourselves that excludes the reality of our biology.

Why are we largely unaware of oxytocin's role in our sexuality?

I first learned about it from *Unprotected: A Campus Psychiatrist Reveals How Political Correctness in Her Profession Endangers Every Student* (Sentinel, the Penguin Group, 2006), a book that was initially published anonymously because it was risky for its author, Miriam Grossman, M.D., to attach her name to it (Penguin republished in 2007).

In *Unprotected*, Dr. Grossman wrote: "Neuroscientists have discovered that specific brain cells and chemicals are involved in attachment." Oxytocin is that chemical. "Moreover, oxytocin increases trust." …"Like it or not, hard science suggests that intimacy initiates a trusting bond." (pp. 7,8,12)

On her website, ONE HUNDRED PERCENT MD, ZERO PERCENT PC, Dr. Grossman writes: "…intimacy has emotional consequences. Science says touch is meaningful and creates feelings of trust and love. We are hard wired to attach."[2]

Why are we not hearing about oxytocin's effect on our sexuality? And why is it not emphasized in the educational materials on sex prepared by colleges for their incoming female *and* male students? We are finally hearing from the #MeToo movement about sexual assaults and unwanted advances, but we are not hearing about oxytocin and its effect on our sexuality.

The fact that we are not, tells you a lot. It tells you that it's not PC.

---

[2] http://www.miriamgrossmanmd.com/ - accessed on September 19, 2019

As Dr. Grossman put it in *Unprotected*:

> I submit that the notion of being designed to bond is to some an unwelcome finding. It implies that sexual activity, especially in women, might be more complex than, say, working out. It suggests that women may be vulnerable, unprotected. ... Women more vulnerable than men? You can't get less politically correct than that. (p. 9) ...
>
> To acknowledge the negative consequences of the anything-goes, hooking-up culture would challenge the notion that women are just like men and undermine the premise of "safer sex." (p. 5)

Years ago, based on her clinical experience, Grossman dared to say what we all know but are not supposed to say: casual sex is more likely to have emotional repercussions for women than it does for men.

Female students were ending up in her office with depression and other psychological symptoms brought on by hook-ups:

> They're lining up for appointments and flooding our phone lines. I've seen so many students like these, they blur together in my mind, a pitiable crowd of confused, vulnerable young women, ill prepared for campus life, making poor choices, and paying high prices. (p. 4)

It stands to reason that young women who don't know about oxytocin and its effects are more likely to leave themselves open to hurt than they might otherwise do, or be less likely to wonder what's wrong with them if they find themselves wanting an emotional attachment after a hook-up.

There's nothing wrong with you if you feel that way.

You are a woman, that's all.

And while everyone is jumping on the Be-Your-Authentic-Self

bandwagon, **why** are young women under pressure to be a PC version of themselves and to think that something is wrong with them if they don't feel like that version? What's up with that?

What *is* up with that?

We don't *have* to be like men in every way. And the fact that we have differences must be acknowledged and respected if we want to make change built on a foundation of truth and reality, whether they fit some wished-for social agenda, or not.

To me, considering women sexually liberated when their sexuality aligns more with men's is the very opposite of considering women equals—as if, to be equal, we must be like men. Why are men still the standard by which we measure ourselves? Why, unless we still consider men superior?

"We can do anything that men can do" has become the slogan of modern Western women. And yes, we can do many of the same things that men do, and this change has promoted extraordinary growth in women and in men. But we *are also* different from men—and, in our ongoing struggle for equality, we have largely ignored and refused to acknowledge how we are different.

Women, over all of Earth, comprise by far the greatest number of individuals who have historically been and continue to be subjected to pervasive abuse of different kinds. Until recently, however, we were relatively brushed off. The #MeToo movement even came later in the victim queue than trans people did—and it has a different focus. It does not challenge the idea that women are and should be more like men. Our liberation is defined in traditionally male terms like power and influence and physical prowess and sitting on boards and the freedom to have strictly physical sex.

That's the PC view of women.

We *had* to get away from our history of oppression. But trying to be like men is just as oppressive. We do not live in our unique feminine power when we try to be like men.

Some of us need the freedom to feel ourselves deeply and truly again—to let go of how we think we are supposed to be or feel. We need to open ourselves to whatever we find, however appealing or unappealing, however PC or not PC. And to interpret that in our lives.

It's time to let go of the paradigm we have accepted and try to live by. Men and women differ in ways that many of us no longer acknowledge, respect, or value.

We certainly differ in more ways than is considered PC.

I am not making anyone wrong or bad. I am simply saying that we are who we are, and we are not free so long as we accept standards of personal freedom that are based on men's biology and that deny and undermine the differences in our natures.

It will make you and the world better if you love yourself.

Can we have the freedom to re-explore who we are?

We do not have that permission now. It's not PC.

> "Of my two 'handicaps' being female put more obstacles in my path than being black."
>
> – Shirley Chisholm, first black woman elected to Congress (1968)
>
> https://www.thoughtco.com/shirley-chisholm-quotes-3530176 - accessed on 11.21.19

17
STICKS & STONES

We used to say, "Sticks and stones can break my bones, but names will never hurt me." Now it's all about names.

A beloved cousin reminded me that the early-PC designation of Ms., instead of Miss or Mrs., felt awkward and odd at first. But it made a difference because women of marriageable age were supposed to be married in those days; if you weren't married, you faced particular kinds of discrimination. Also, using Ms. simplifed things for everyone.

Did we get equal pay for equal work from that name change, though? Nope. An end to physical or sexual harrassment and abuse? Nope. An end to domestic violence and trafficking of women? Nope.

Ms. is just a name. It can't do those things. Equality for women will take massive commitment and effort—as does other real change.

PC arose in response to the way many individuals and groups were marginalized, discriminated against, and oppressed. I appreciate that. It is right and respectful to call people by the names they choose.

But names are not inclusion. And names have begun to complicate and splinter, while the designation of Ms. simplified things.

Language is important. Names are important. It is also important to recognize what names can and cannot do. And to recognize that designations that are sliced and diced into finer and finer bits can divide rather than unite.

18
THE GREAT OZ OF OUR TIME

Will has become the Great Oz of our time—our magical mystery wizard. Shazaam—we have willed it, and it is so!

Whatever we say is true, is true.

And nothing else.

But our wills were not designed to do the work of creation, of nature, no matter how much we will them to. Will cannot exceed human limits; we cannot bend everything to it. Will and intention can be astonishing and truly transformative, but we are still biological creatures. And we cannot will ourselves to sleep, have an orgasm, or be a giraffe.

With great fanfare and hope, we now declare ourselves to be a creation of our own choosing. We are whatever we say we are (in social and gender realms—not in the racial realm). No one is legally or socially allowed to question that. No one else, nothing else, may define us. This is a core tenet of PC, and any other view is automatically considered prejudiced and hateful. But behind this enthralling, ever-changing reality, we remain human beings, tied to truths that are not subject to our will.

Will is not a god. Or even a wizard. And neither are we.

Used for work it cannot do, will is a hoax.

The *You-Are-Anything-You-Say-You-Are* movement (which I think is a child of the human potential movement, the *You-Can-Be-Anything-You-Want-to-Be-or-Anything-You-Can-Dream-of* movement) has become our cultural worldview. And it has been enormously helpful to many people, who had been limited in all kinds of ridiculous ways.

But it has also become extreme. Now, anything is supposed to be possible, and reality is whatever we say it is, and *only* what we say it is. Truth and reality are relative—we call them "our truths." This is helpful because it recognizes that our views come from our backgrounds, perceptions, experiences, etc., and that someone else holds different views, which come from theirs.

But is everything relative now? Is anything inherently true?

Asking this is not PC and is not allowed.

When we bend all truth and reality to our wills, however, there's no compass for our world anymore—no up, no down—no orientation at all. Because reality can at any and every turn be constructed and construed as we want it to be.

These days, biology is viewed with suspicion—as if it is some false, old-school notion, and discounted—except, of course, when it comes to race, and then it becomes a line we cannot cross. When it comes to race and ethnicity, we go looking for our biology: our genealogy.

I am painfully aware that biology has been misused to hurt some people, such as Blacks and Jews and gays. But I question why socially constructed reality—the reality that people create for themselves and decide is true—is the only reality we now consider valid.

If we don't honestly acknowledge and address what's in our DNA, we cannot adequately address the things we want to change because we do not understand ourselves. And we cannot value their presence in us as a tool of survival. Incorrect analysis of an issue or problem cannot lead to a successful solution. I was taught that as a graduate student in social policy, but it's really just common sense.

For example, diversity has always been at the core of my life. And when I was doing some research for *Different: Our Universal Longing for Community* (2016), I came upon some very disturbing and unwelcome research conducted at Yale University's Infant Cognition Center, which clearly shows that *infants* prefer sameness to difference. In other words, children don't have to be taught, as was long thought, to prefer sameness: prejudicial teaching occurs *on top* of the biological layer we are given.

And I finally realized that, as much as I didn't want this to be true (and it isn't for about 15% of the infants observed), it makes sense that we would be predisposed to stick with the familiar when you think about our ancestors roaming the African veldt in groups and coming across other groups ("outsiders") who might be foes. In other words, this is part of our nature, *and* it has been vital in our survival as a species. Now, if we want to overcome the problems we have in relation to diversity ("birds of a feather..."), and it is imperative to do so in our increasingly shrinking and interconnected world, we have to take our biology into account. We need to "friend" ourselves and each other as we are, not just as we wish to be. If we do, and only if we do, I believe we can make a different kind of progress than we can make with PC—than we can make by considering others bad and wrong. We will come from love and understanding, possibly even humor: "Oh crap, that ancient thing in us is here again. Am I doing that again? Are they doing that again?"

It's us, like it or not. It's part of who we are. And it served our species for a long, long time. It's just not working well for us now.

It's not good or bad.

It just is.

It's one of our ancient struggles.

Different is just different. It is neither worse nor better.

Whenever you feel yourself going to any attitude of prejudice in yourself, think O*h, that old thing is back again?* Don't try to will it away. Just laugh and let it go.

Don't grow it with PC's angry, hypersensitive, humorless, ready-to-be-offended energy.

It's plenty big already.

And remember, will has limits.

Because we're human.

19
KITTEN EARS

One day, at a job in NYC where there was a dress code, a young woamn came in wearing one of those kitten-ear headbands.

It was cute, but inappropriate for a professional setting, and several of us noticed it. We found out that she was a new intern who had come to have her picture (with the ears on) taken for her photo ID.

One of my superiors said that the intern would be told nicely to remove the kitten ears *if* she wore them because she thought they were cute. But *if she actually identified as a cat*, we would have to check EEO law to see if she could be asked to remove her kitten ears for work because it might not be PC.

I wish I had made this up.

20

IF TRANSGENDER, WHY NOT TRANS-RACE?

Let's get right to this. No Black person I know would put up with someone White, who identifies Black, claiming to be Black (or vice versa). We have already seen that happen in the case of Rachel Dolezal, a White woman who was president of the NAACP chapter in Spokane, Washington, who posed as Black.

Black folks and other folks of color experience daily insults that you don't experience if you are White, no matter how you feel or identify. Likewise, White folks are unlikely to accept that someone who is not White actually is White because they say they identify White.

People are not walking around saying they were born into the wrong racial body. This will not become a movement. No sir. Can you imagine a White person running around saying they were born into the wrong body—they are really Asian? Or they identify as Asian, so they are? No. (Many folks are mixed-race, of course, and identify in various ways.)

In the *Rachel Divide* (a 2018 Neflix documentary about Dolezal), Latoya Brackett, a Black woman who is only identified in the film as an NAACP member, says: "Transracial is the epitome of White privilege. If every ethnic group cannot do that in the same capacity and be received in that manner, then it's a privilege." Another Black woman in the

Rachel Divide says, "You can't just appropriate persecution because it's 'cool.'" And, on *The Real*, the TV talk show where Dolezal appeared, a Black panelist (whose name I didn't catch) said, "She makes it sound like you can pick your race."

Exactly. And people generally don't buy that.

But we can now pick our gender. In fact, we are encouraged to. Some states now allow parents to leave the gender designation blank on their newborn's birth certificate.

Why is transgender embraced and trans-race forbidden?

In the *Rachel Divide*, a transsexual Black woman is asked how transsexual is different from trans-racial. She says it is "completely" different because, "[Dolezal's] blackness is a performance. Our trans-ness is our identity."

But how is Dolezal's identification as a Black person (if that's how she genuinely identifies) different from identifying as someone of the opposite gender? What makes one of them more real?

At one point, Dolezal asks: "Do we have the right to live exactly as we feel?"

It's the question of the day.

What I don't understand is why we seem to be *leading* our children— in some states and places—to question their gender identity. We're not waiting for *them* to say something, or to grow up. We talk and teach transgender in school, where our kids often don't even learn correct English or sufficient science. It's the PC thing to do.

But *why* is it the PC thing to do? I spent months trying to understand why we regard transgender and trans-racial identity so differently. The answer was not self-evident to me when I began to really think about it.

Near the end of the *Rachel Divide*, someone off-camera (I assume it was the film's director Laura Brownson) asks Dolezal, "At what point does identity trump reality?" Adding that Black people have spoken (in the film), she then says, "Ultimately, Black people govern blackness."

Do you agree?

If so, then who governs gender? Why don't biological women and men govern their genders?

There have always been individuals who do not feel that their assigned gender fits them. They have struggled for acceptance; they have been murdered; they are terrified; and I want them to be safe and happy. They should be able to live freely as they feel themselves to be and be included in our society, lovingly and without prejudice.

What I don't understand is the need for the wholesale movement we now have, which seems to sow doubt and confusion, in the name of freedom and rights, in the minds of kids who weren't questioning their identities and never exhibited or expressed discomfort with the gender they were assigned at birth.

Why are we going out of our way to encourage our children to think about whether to be a boy or a girl or some mixture, instead of waiting to see if *they* have an issue?

To backtrack for a moment, as I understand it, Dolezal offends Black folks because one cannot simply appropriate oppression. *They* govern blackness, and trans-racial does not fly with them.

Does every group govern its identity? If you are a White man, for example, do you govern (and define) what that is? Or is there a relationship between being oppressed and governing one's identity?

In thinking about this, I realized that women—roughly half of the world's population and *by far* the greatest number of historically subjugated people—have not said, "Hey, you can't claim to be a woman if you don't go through what a woman goes through."

And, speaking for a moment as a biological woman, trans women do not experience the monthly cycles and hormonal roller-coaster that men ridicule us for, or get fibroids, which cause many of us pain and danger. Trans women cannot get ovarian or uterine cancer, or have the ability to bear children and all that comes with it, including, sometimes, death. Being a biological woman comes with a host of complex physical realities that are not easy or fun—that can be very challenging and involve a whole lot more than how you look and feel about yourself.

I have no problem with anyone identifying as a trans woman, but if you are not subject to the biological vulnerabilities that biological women do, please do not insist that I call you a "real" woman. And how is it fair for biological women to have to compete in athletic events with trans women, who often beat them because of their biology?

I also wonder why is it OK for (what used to be called) "drag queens" to caricature women when it's not OK for women to parody trans people. We approach trans with a preciousness I have never seen.

I love it when comics make fun of women and men and are spot-on. But I, personally, do not enjoy it when someone takes on a complete, exaggerated female persona and parodies women. Men are not parodied that way. Nor are trans people.

And if I were to put on black-face, you know exactly what would happen.

What's interesting to me is that biological women don't object.

Why? Because it wouldn't be nice? Wouldn't be PC? Because every woman except me really enjoys it?

Black folks govern blackness, but biological women don't govern woman-ness. And biological men don't govern man-ness. No one, according to the PC point of view as I understand it, governs gender except the individual who identifies as one or the other.

Gender is far deeper and more primary than race. We could be human without evolving into different races, but we would not have survived as a species without gender. It is our fundamental division.

However you identify, be well, be happy, go live. I am *not* saying—I am *never* saying—that we should be mean to each other. I am saying that we need to accept one another and our differences, practice the Golden Rule, and include everyone in our human circle. If you don't feel like yourself in the body you were born into, do what you need to do to feel like yourself. You are a valued member of the human family.

I am not making you wrong.

But it is also not wrong for the rest of us to be curious, even in ways you might object to. It is simply human. Without curiosity, we would not have survived as a species. And curiosity about gender is as fundamental as it gets. You say you're this, not that. OK. Then we naturally want to know what "that" is. It's part of being biological creatures. It's part of being alive. It's part of what I meant in "The Great

Oz of our time" about the irrelevance of biology these days, about the purely social construction of being, about the role that *will* now plays in our lives.

But I am not allowed to say that. I don't govern transgender.

Trans folks do.

And, while I recognize the life-threatening and self-threatening perils they have historically endured, and their need to hide, I ask them to appreciate and respect that biological women, too, have always faced life-threatening and self-threatening perils.

And, like Black folks, we generally can't or don't hide.

We're just out there.

But to get back to my original question, I was about to give up on understanding why transgender is encouraged and trans-race is forbidden. Then I came across *Unprotected: A Campus Psychiatrist Reveals How Political Correctness in Her Profession Endangers Every Student,*[3] by Dr. Miriam Grossman, which I mentioned in my earlier chapter on the PC woman. In it, Dr. Grossman describes the sex ed information that the university where she worked prepared for their students, which include(d) information on bestiality, "golden showers," how to clean an instrument that had been bloodied in a sadistic sexual encounter, etc. And suddenly, I felt I understood: *PC's stance on sex is that sexual exploration and activity of any and all kinds is encouraged. It's considered necessary and healthy, as long as it is concensual and we practice "safe sex."*

But "anything goes" has never applied to race. Ohhh, noo.

The PC eagerness to embrace and endorse all forms of sexuality and sexual preferences is what has led not only to acceptance of transgender individuals—who undertake the most fundamental transformation of identity possible—but to a movement toward transgender and all forms of gender nonconformity.

This is why we can choose our gender identities, but not our racial

---

[3] *Unprotected* was originally published in 2006 by Sentinel Books, by "Anonymous, M.D." because Grossman's career would likely have been jeopardized. It was republished with the correct attribution in 2007.

ones. Black folks and other people of color ain't havin' it. (Nor are White folks.) And they govern race.

I don't know or care if Dr. Grossman is considered a right-winger by some. To me, what's true is true, no matter who says it.

True is true, whether I like it or not. Or whether you do.

As I said, this book is not a safe space—for you *or* for me.

Dr. Grossman decries "activists who value social change more than truth."[4] I believe in social change based on truth.

---

[4] http://www.miriamgrossmanmd.com/ - accessed on July 28, 2019

21
TRANS-BOTS

One other thing: I am haunted by my gut feeling that the thrust to neutralize gender—to do away with it—is tied to our ever more roboticized world of artifical intelligence (AI).

We are robotically connected to our phones, processing an avalanche of information while our hearts seem increasingly absent from our interactions with other human beings (except during times of crisis). More and more robotic devices are in our homes and pass on information about us to the tech giants and their partners (and sometimes, as we saw recently, to other people). We blithely give Google and FB and other tech giants permission to use our information without thinking about it because we care more about convenience than privacy, because we don't want to bother reading the lengthy disclosure statements, and because we just want the access and ease that it gives us.

More and more, robots are made to do the work of humans. And they do not need gender to procreate.

More and more, we do not need gender to procreate, either.

I am convinced of a direct link between the push to advance AI and the push to obliterate gender.

I bet someone will make a lot of money from this. And it will not be the trans folks.

22
REDNECKS, CRACKERS & WHITE TRASH

So, why is it still OK to call people "rednecks" and "crackers" and "trailer trash" (the least privileged of White people), though we are not allowed to call anyone else pejorative names? People I know will even laugh if you do, because we *know* that all those guys are racist and stupid and voted for Trump. We are perfectly free to deride them.

For most of US history, White people (especially men) were supposedly better. They ran the country and still do. Moreover, those of us who are White continue to reap the benefits of White skin privilege every day and in *many* ways. This is just true.

It is also true that, while we cannot say or even think a "wrong" word about anyone in the protected categories, we are free to disdain the people we consider rednecks, crackers, trailer trash, or White trash. We passionately and indignantly exclude the people we feel better than, because we know that they're deplorable, though many or most of us have not talked to them.

Inclusion does not include them. And it does not include Trump supporters.

They are the new outsiders, the only people we can and are even expected to scorn. We do not want to talk or listen to those people. And we think we don't need to. We think we already know *what* they are.

Someone once asked me if I think PC keeps things civil. I don't think that PC does anything genuine to promote race or other relations. I think it maintains a pretense of that, while the real stuff goes on underneath.

PC is just a Band-Aid that covers the *ouch* of our universal difficulty with diversity.

And Band-Aids hurt when they are ripped off.

This Band-Aid has already come off. And it hurts like hell.

We see fists. Guns. Racially motivated murders and openly racial slurs. Rage and backlash. The deep divisions between us.

Progressives take no responsibility for our part in creating—partly through PC—the circumstances that led to Trump's election. They do not see the divisions and backlash as anything we might have helped to bring about. But it is no more righteous for us to include some groups and exclude others than it is for the rightwing to do that with people they don't like. We think we're superior because we think we're inclusive. *But we only include the people we agree with, and we especially love them if they are victims.* And why is it fine to feel better than all White men, when it was not acceptable for them to feel that way?

We seem to have no intention of finding common ground anymore. We're holed up in our self-righteous thought trenches, and they're holed up in theirs.

In January 2019, I moved from Harlem to North Carolina. Some friends were shocked that I would move to the South. One repeatedly told me to turn it into a blue state. Some said things like "Aw shucks" or "Sho' nuff." I couldn't stand the smug, superior attitude. But it took a while for me to remember that I had been that self-righteous lefty with a woman from Alabama when I was in Newark and scorned White Southerners in principle, and from up there on my very high horse. I didn't even bother to find out that she, who is now a close friend, had risked her life, multiple times and in many ways, for civil rights.

Now that I've moved to an area that many Northerners are moving to, I frequently see them telling Southerners how to do things. Some indigenous Southerners even have bumper stickers to the effect that they do not need Northerners to tell them how things are done. In Cary, N.C., which is locally referred to as the Containment Area for Retired Yankees (C-A-R-Y), Northerners have created a mini New York because they want things to be like NYC. And one friend warned me not to go to a nearby town because it is "the Old South," where "everyone is snaggle-toothed." (I spent a wonderful day there with another friend from the North.) I have not seen Southerners do this with Northerners, although I imagine it occurs. But Northerners do not even seem to notice or question their superior, knee-jerk attitude toward Southerners—though we all know there would be (and should be) a huge outcry if they were to treat folks in one of the PC groups that way.

After a nasty incident in the community where I now live, I surprised myself by suddenly speaking up. It was like my mouth just started talking without me. And it asked folks if they wanted to have a country—and said that if they do, we have to figure out how to talk to each other. It also suggested that they read *Strangers in Their Own Land: Anger and Mourning on the American Right* (The New Press, 2016), a National Book Award finalist. The author, sociologist Arlie Russell Hochschild, traveled to Louisiana from her Berkeley home to talk to people about why they had joined the Tea Party, and why there is such an absolute failure of empathy—what she refers to as an "empathy wall"—between people with different beliefs who don't belong to the same political party: our "Great Divide." If you haven't read her book, I urge you to, whatever your political beliefs.

We have to decide if we want to remain a nation, and what that can look like. Is it more important to us to stay in our well-worn thought trenches or be willing to listen to someone with a different point of view?

We need to listen, not just tell. That goes for all of us.

White males, Southerners, and Trump supporters are the outgroups these days. You can consider this justice served, if you want, given our history, but it is not viable. It will not work.

Respect must apply to everyone. Period.

"When you show deep empathy toward others, their defensive energy goes down, and positive energy replaces it. That's when you can get more creative in solving problems."

— Stephen Covey

- accessed 11.21.19

And do not underestimate the degree to which the rightwing *and* the liberal media control what we think and know. They scream and frighten, sow division, hyperbolize—even about ridiculous things like an insignificant snowfall. Did you know it's slippery? Wow! That's news! Those things were considered a normal part of life when I was growing up—no one interviewed people on the six o-clock news about how they felt about some snow.

And then there are the bigger issues. In all my years as an activist, I never saw an event accurately reported that I had attended. And Joy told me she knows reporters who are told to change the story they submit.

Everything is filtered and spun according to the outlet's point of view and intended audience. Everything is colored by the political lens through which an event is viewed. It seems less and less possible for people to be able to consider—or even care about—separating their preconceived mindset from how they might view an event.

Both sides of the press daily aggravate our tensions and divisions—for their own power, it seems. I can't help it if Trump says this, and he only says it about the liberal press.

The press has become a primary and self-serving instrument of division. The truth we know is what we receive through the channels whose filters we choose to believe.

Take a closer look, turn the kaleidoscope a notch, and think about what you see.

23
THEY'RE NOT TRUMP

Trump supporters are no more Trump than I am Obama just because I voted for Obama. I have been trying to point out this lack of logic to friends. *Certainly*, some of Trump's supporters are racist—very racist—maybe even many. But always, always, we need to reserve judgment about individuals till we know *who* they are.

Today (August 2, 2019), a friend sent me the following quote from "We're All Tired of Being Called Racists," in *The Atlantic* (August 2, 2019), by Elaina Plott, a staff writer at the magazine. Plott, who attended a Trump rally in Cincinnati the night before, spoke to some attendees afterward, and reported that what:

> …the rally-goers I spoke to last night seemed most nonplussed by—not so much that Trump had been roundly condemned in recent days as a racist, or a bigot, but that they, by virtue of association, had been as well. But rather than distancing them from Trump, the accusations have only seemed to strengthen their support of this president. *To back down, they suggested, would be to bow down to the scourge of political correctness."* (my italics added) …

One man told Plott that he had spent fifteen years working with impoverished children in Thailand and had seen "real" racism; a woman told Plott that eight of her thirteen grandchildren are mixed-race and much beloved.

The definition of racism has come to mean what PC means by it, and racist means, as one friend said, "anyone who doesn't subscribe to the far-left point of view."

I have seen racism in many subtle and systemic forms that White people usually do not see, and I understand why people of color (or lefties) might reject the way these Trump supporters describe racism. The way many White people define racism is very simple—as simple as whether they use the n-word. They do not compute or include an understanding of systemic racism, its reach or consequences. But could we please stop with our criticism for just a minute and *listen to their hearts? With our hearts?* Do you have *a heart* for anyone who believes other than you do?

"We honor cultural identity. We always have; we always will. But separatism is not allowed. Separatism is not the American way. We must not allow ideas like political correctness to divide us and cause us to reverse hard-won achievements in human rights and civil rights."

– Barbara Jordan, first Black woman from the Deep South to be elected to the House of Representatives (1972-1978), from her keynote speech in 1992 to the Democratic National Convention

http://gos.sbc.edu/j/jordan2.html - accessed 11.19.19

24
STRAIGHT UP

These days, I prefer to talk and listen to anyone who is straight up with me. No matter what they think.

I'm ready to do that, and I know we can talk to each other if we really want to, because I have seen it. But it will be difficult, and we need to have the will and the courage for it.

I'm Jewish by heritage. Some people automatically hate me for that. Maybe you do. People have all kinds of stereotypes about Jews, some of which are based on reality. But what do you know about *me*, personally? Have *I* done anything to you? And what do *I* really know about *you*, just because some people call you a redneck or a nigger? We will never know what's true about other people unless we become more interested in exploring who they are than in assuming we already know.

Let's see *who* I think you are and who you think I am, not who we have decided we are before even meeting each other. Time and again, we think we know who someone is. Time and again, uncomfortable conversations have opened doors to understanding and mutual respect that no one thought possible, let alone the participants themselves.

But real conversations and change cannot take place in a culture that prohibits honesty if that's not PC, and where people are more interested in sticking to what they have always thought and want to continue to think than they are in listening to anyone who doesn't see things their way.

We are deeply mired in our own thought grooves.

We are afraid. And we are stuck.

If we want to have a nation (do we? it's a real question), we need to talk about a lot of hard stuff and include the people we disagree with.

Yes, there is a White backlash and White resentment at becoming a majority minority country. The same fear and resistance generally attend major shifts in any population, community, demographic. *This reaction is as old as human time.* It is something we need to work to overcome because it is human at a primal level. The people who face change and hate it—the people you call racist or sexist or homophobic—need to be understood as human, not demonized.

You could be them in another context, about other people.
Do not kid yourself.

In a courageous documentary, *The White Right: Facing the Enemy* (released by Netflix in 2018), activist and filmmaker Deeyah Khan—a Muslim woman of color—"decided to meet people who think the White race is under threat, and that I'm their enemy. I wanted to see if I could understand their anger—to get to know the personal reasons why they are drawn to such hatred and division… I wanted to find out what they're really like as human beings."

It probably helped for her to be a woman, and a young and beautiful one at that, but still, some of the men she got to know changed their views of her and of Muslims during the filming. Not all of them, for sure, but it was very moving. The takeaway was that racial hatred often comes from deep personal pain and hurt, and that when people get to know each other as individuals, their hate often melts. We know that, we've seen that, time and again, and we need to remember it.[5]

If we engage with people we fear and hate, we may not get far. For example, one of the guys Khan interviewed grew to like her—but continued to insist that all Jews and homosexuals should be killed. But change—or at least understanding—happens often enough that I, for one, want to pursue it. The real question isn't whether it will produce results, but whether we even want to try to talk to each other honestly

---

[5] For inspiration, I suggest *The Best of Enemies,* a true story.

and openly. Do we have the will for that, the heart, the hope, the interest, and the willingness to *listen*? Do we even *want* to understand?

Or are we more interested in feeling right and righteous and staying in our safe spaces, where everyone thinks like we do?

This is not essentially a political question. It's a social one.

And it applies to all of us.

25

A GREAT TOOL FOR THE GREAT DIVIDE

Who benefits from PC?

Do you?

Are you sure?

Identity politics and PC have not only been a major contributor to the divide we face—they have also been a major distraction from the growing divide between haves and have-nots, and from the encroachment of interests into our lives that do not have our interests at heart. Identity politics and PC keep us focused on mini offenses instead of the big picture. Meanwhile, colossal corruption and injustices flourish—the massive, intentional destruction of other human beings for money, for power.

Our humanity is slipping away while we have fits over our identity—while we fuss over whether we belong to this category or that or need to create something new because we really don't fit anywhere, now that we think about it.

Humanity is not identity. Humanity belongs to our entire species. It is our compassion, our kindness, our willingness to help and consider others (*all* others, including people we disagree with or don't like).

When you have that attitude, you are not just waiting to be offended.

We have come apart. We are a nation in descent, and we are failing.

Everyone I know is stressed to the max, worried about health insurance, working their butts off, worried about the future.

And nothing has changed for the kids in the projects.

If we want respect, we must be respectful. Truly respectful. And *truly* inclusive if we claim to be inclusive. And we need to stop using language to pretend things that just aren't so.

How about making it more important to find out about each other than staying in our familiar protected tents, flaps down? We have stopped exploring others if they are outside our tents and fall into "bad" categories. We are busy being right and better and congratulating ourselves.

We do not venture outside our own safe spaces.

We just blast away blindly at the big bad bear we think we know is out there.

Sometimes, since I started thinking about PC, I feel like I'm on a trip with no end. It seems to be the nature of PC that it is always changing. Why does the horizon we chase keep moving away? Why is our quest for—what?—seemingly never ending? We are always looking for new victims. We are splitting more and more hairs. With gender, we have gone as far as we can go. I am curious to see what comes next. What *can* come next?

It used to be considered important and right to listen to someone else's opinion. It was expected. It was part of how we learned. Part of how we were supposed to treat others and be in the world. Now it's considered wrong to listen—listen truly—unless their opinion is like our own.

PC has played a *major* role in creating and growing this divisive, immature, and unhelpful stance—this world in which we should not listen to each other unless we already basically agree.

Meanwhile, the chasm between the very rich and powerful, and the rest of us, continues to grow. Meanwhile, a totally corrupt system continues to benefit from our focus on identity and PC issues. Meanwhile, robotics is creating the greatest challenge humankind has ever faced, as Stephen Hawking, the renowned physicist, said.[6] Meanwhile, Earth suffers from our strife, and makes us suffer.

We need to broaden our focus and shift what energizes us. Find meaning and purpose. Notice what's bigger than we are. Help others— and not just people you consider victims. It's the best antidote I know for obsessive self-involvement, feeling like a victim, and waiting to be offended.

We need each other.

---

[6] https://www.cnbc.com/2017/11/06/stephen-hawking-ai-could-be-worst-event-in-civilization.html WATCH: Stephen Hawking: AI will 'transform or destroy' society

26
PC VS. INCLUSION

Inclusion is what I want—PC is what I want to be liberated from.

Inclusion is genuinely loving and accepting. It includes *everyone* in the human circle. Everyone belongs in it and is welcome. Inclusion is not a dogma or construct; it does not preach; it is not victim-based; it does not set forth precise prescriptions for our interactions, behavior, and speech. Inclusion is easy-going and open and does not make a federal case out of everything.

It does not rest on blame and offense. Or defense.

What we need is simple:

We don't need to like each other.

We don't need to agree with each other.

We just need to respect each other, include each other, and practice the Golden Rule—no exceptions.

That's all.

I invite you to drop PC. It isn't inclusion. It isn't real respect. And it certainly isn't the Golden Rule because it doesn't apply to everyone.

It has become a gag order.

And it stands squarely in the way of inclusion, though it pretends otherwise. Not only does PC select who gets to be included in our circle of the righteous—it interferes with genuine communication and surrounds the idea of difference with darkness, vise-like control, and humorlessness; and it continues and promotes a simplistic idea of good guys and bad guys, based solely on their beliefs and their *whats*. Not their character. Not their *whos*. No one with the wrong beliefs or creds will be included.

Oh no.

That wouldn't be PC at all.

27
IN THE END

I have learned that our minds can be the most impenetrable prison of all, or our greatest ally and sometimes our only freedom.

I have learned that internal freedom is the only freedom that can never be taken away. It is its own private space, and you won't get to it through PC.

I have learned that you cannot feel free or be free and feel like a victim; they are opposites.

And I have learned that the choice is ours.

Remember:
"Love is the energy that comes directly from our integrity—from who we really are."
- Joy

And know that:
This book carries my love to you.

28
NOW WHAT?

This page is intentionally left blank.

ACKNOWLEDGMENTS

Thanks to the wonderful people, who helped me, variously, with the title, thinking about the contents, and all the myriad things that inevitably arise when one is putting a book together. Special thanks to Joy and Bob, without whom this book would never have come to be, and I would have continued to be less than I am. Tremendous gratitude to Ayo for letting me interview her and include this necessarily shortened version of our conversation. And thanks to Marita Rivero for letting me include part of my interview with her for my first book, *Different.*

Much appreciation to Sandra Santana for initial help with formatting, and to my son Calien for his feedback and thoughts on the title and concept. Many thanks to Tamasin Sterner for reading an early draft, and ginormous thanks to Susan Gevertz for reading the final draft and offering spot-on and insightful comments. To my cover designer and my illustrator, a big smile and a hug of gratitude!

Thank you, too, for the gift of MLK, Jr., who always amazes me; for Brené Brown, whose talks helped me to "dare greatly" and take this risk; for Bill Maher, who took on PC when no one else would, and continues to; and to my PCP—Jennifer McCauley, MD—for remarking on something I said, which I then added to my Dedication.

For the vast and unbelievably generous amount of time, wisdom, smarts, and marketing assistance that Louise Vogel contributed, I do not have adequate words, but I will forever be grateful. She is an incredible friend and helped to birth this book in the final, struggling stages of its development.

Thanks to you all for reading and thinking.

And, always, thanks to Spirit.

ABOUT THE AUTHOR

This is Corinna's second book. Her first—*Different: Our Universal Longing for Community*—is an honest, interview-based conversation about race, class, and our universal difficulty with all difference. It is set at Lincoln University, the first Historically Black College/University, and the adjoining poor community. Corinna grew up in both.

The daughter of parents whose families were killed by Nazis, Corinna's lifelong commitment to diversity and inclusion led to multiple arrests for civil rights in the '60s. In 1967, she was living in the Black community in Newark, NJ, working as an organizer; when the city exploded, she and her friends had to sleep in the bathtub to avoid the National Guard's bullets.

A professional writer and editor since 1995, when she co-authored a field research report for the Library of Congress, Corinna has held editorial positions at Columbia University, the City University of New York's School of Professional Studies, and a variety of nonprofits, public agencies, and non-governmental organizations. After fifty years in New York City—the last twenty-five of which were lived in Harlem, where she worked with kids in public housing to give voice to their stories—Corinna moved to North Carolina in 2019. She facilitates discussions on race and community and continues to write and edit on a freelance basis.

www.CorinnaFalesConsulting.com

Made in the USA
Columbia, SC
29 February 2020